The BEST PLACES TO KISS Cookbook

CAROL FRIEBERG

Recipes from the Most Romantic Restaurants, Cafés, and Inns of the Pacific Northwest

SASQUATCH BOOKS
SEATTLE

"Orecchiette Salad with Roasted Beets and Fennel" (p. 58) is reprinted from *Macrina Bakery & Cafe Cookbook* by Leslie Mackie, © 2003 by Leslie Mackie, published by Sasquatch Books.

"Chocolate Pavé" (p. 115) is reprinted from *Christina's Cookbook* by Christina Orchid, © 2004 by Christina Orchid, published by Sasquatch Books.

Printed in Canada
Published by Sasquatch Books
Distributed by PGW/Perseus
15 14 13 12 11 10 09 08   9 8 7 6 5 4 3 2 1

Text by: Carol Frieberg
Cover photograph (bottom): © iStockphoto.com/Joe Brandt
Cover photographs (top): Lara Ferroni
Cover design: Sasquatch Books
Interior design and composition: Kate Basart/Union Pageworks
Interior photographs: Lara Ferroni

Library of Congress Cataloging-in-Publication Data
Frieberg, Carol, 1959-
   The best places to kiss cookbook : recipes from the most romantic restaurants, cafés, and inns of the Pacific Northwest / by Carol Frieberg. — 1st ed.
      p. cm.
Includes index.
ISBN-13: 978-1-57061-563-4
ISBN-10: 1-57061-563-2
1. Cookery. 2. Cookery, American—Pacific Northwest style. I. Title.
TX714.F7447 2008
641.5795 —dc22
            2008013758

Sasquatch Books | 119 South Main Street, Suite 400 | Seattle, WA 98104
206/467-4300 | www.sasquatchbooks.com | custserv@sasquatchbooks.com

Never underestimate the power of a kiss.

Contents

Salads 45

Main Courses 61

Desserts 101

Acknowledgments

Each one of these recipes has a special story for me. The following friends (and friends of friends) graciously volunteered their time, kitchens, and families to help evaluate and make suggestions for the recipes in this book. My heartfelt thanks to you all.

Kate Bochert

Diane Carlson

Julie Christensen

Isabel Church

Diana Clay

Lindsay Colitses

Susan Dunbar

Sally Dupree

Lisa Enriquez

Lori Fox

Barbara Frieberg

Ingrid Gangestad

Julie Jacobson

Carol Janowicz

Jeanne Judd

Cindy Lund

Patti and Terry Mahon

Marc and Jean Oplinger

Julie and Tom Paulson

Linda Roberts

Pat Shanahan

Dawn Thiede

Brad and Mary Beth Wressell

Pam Zacharias

A special thank you to Jeff, for your amazing support—for patiently putting up with my late nights, late dinners, and countless delicious calories!

Introduction

The Fine Art of Cooking and Kissing

The Pacific Northwest has great places to kiss—and to eat! Anyone who is familiar with *The Best Places to Kiss in the Northwest* travel guide knows it's the quintessential resource for romantic destinations in the Pacific Northwest. *The Best Places to Kiss Cookbook* offers up recipes from establishments featured in the 9th and 10th editions of the guidebook. These mood-setting dishes demonstrate what makes those places so romantically celebrated. Dishes you so enjoy when eating out can now easily be prepared at home.

The recipes here capture the adventurous spirit of Northwest chefs and reflect the characteristic flavors of our region—marionberries, apples, pears, hazelnuts, oysters, mussels, salmon, and Dungeness crab, among others. Our Pacific Northwest has emerged as a food and wine destination with its own signature style—fresh, seasonal, local ingredients served with a Pacific Rim flair that is gaining popularity among locals, visitors to the area, and discriminating food critics.

Each recipe boasts local flavor and personality. At the Inn on Orcas Island, breakfast starts the night before, with Washington pears that are poached in a chardonnay syrup, chilled overnight, then served for breakfast with a dollop of creamy ricotta cheese (page 4). On Friday Harbor at The Place Bar & Grill, buckets of Westcott Bay oysters are gathered, then they are roasted with hazelnut butter and served on a bed of salt with a wedge of lemon (page 40). And at Vin Du Lac winery in Lake Chelan, chicken is smoked over applewood, then shredded and piled on baguettes with Havarti cheese and fresh jalapeños (page 66), and enjoyed with a glass of Barrel Select chardonnay.

Complex flavors delight your palate, and recipes that do not require complex preparations are even better! This is not a collection of "chef's recipes" that make for an interesting read but would never be attempted in a home kitchen. You will not have to run to four stores to gather ingredients to prepare these recipes. These recipes are doable as well as delicious. Dishes like Garlic Shrimp Pasta (page 80) and Sizzling Mussels (page 42) are quick to prepare and perfect for a simple romantic evening at home, just the two of you. Toss some simple greens for a salad and, to up the romance, for dessert serve to-die-for Port Truffles (page 123) or a warm slice of Pear and Almond Torte (page 117) with vanilla bean ice cream. What a tasty way to celebrate the end of a day together—or to start a perfect evening.

May you come to enjoy and savor the dishes from the *Best Places to Kiss* and find them so delicious that you'll make them again and again—whenever you want to make something special for someone special. Bon appétit!

—CAROL FRIEBERG, MAY 2008

Breakfast & Brunch

Marionberry Smoothie	*Spring Bay Inn*
Cranberry-Raspberry Fruit Soup	*Boreas Bed & Breakfast Inn*
Chardonnay-Poached Pears	*Inn on Orcas Island*
Granola with Honey Mascarpone	*The Tuwanek Hotel*
Baked Apple Oatmeal	*Selah Inn Bed & Breakfast*
Savory Swiss Scones	*Brookside Inn*
Warm Scones with Apricot-Ginger Jam	*Mt. Hood Hamlet Bed and Breakfast*
Seven-in-One Buttermilk Scones	*The James House*
Pecan Pie Mini Muffins	*Channel House*
Magnificent Bran Muffins	*Halfmoon Bay Cabin*
Walnut and Black Pepper Biscotti	*Patit Creek Restaurant*
Scottish Granola Bars	*The Aerie Resort & Spa*
Ginger and Lemon Pear Pancakes	*Villa Marco Polo Inn*
Bubbly Waffles	*Miller Tree Inn*
Orange Croissant French Toast	*Husum Highlands Bed & Breakfast*
Baked Blueberry-Pecan French Toast	*Autumn Leaves Bed and Breakfast*
Dreamy Brûlée French Toast	*The DreamGiver's Inn*
Cheese Blintz Soufflé with Warm Blueberry Sauce	*A Cowslip's Belle Bed & Breakfast*
Feta, Basil, and Tomato Pie	*Salisbury House*
Chicken and Asparagus Crepes	*English Bay Inn*
Oregon Dungeness Crab Quiche	*Pine Ridge Inn*
Baked Eggs with Gruyère, Tarragon, and Leeks	*Lighthouse Bed and Breakfast*
Asparagus Frittata	*Eagle Rock Lodge*
Mom's Cheddar Baked Eggs	*Salt Spring Vineyards Bed and Breakfast*
Lox Benedict with Lemon-Caper Sauce	*Lost Mountain Lodge*
Pesto Breakfast Quesadillas	*Morgan Hill Retreat*

Marionberry Smoothie

SPRING BAY INN, OLGA, WA   **2 SERVINGS**

Very simple, very quick, and especially refreshing after a morning hike or kayak tour. Marionberries are a blackberry hybrid. If you are lucky enough to have wild blackberries growing in your neighborhood, try making a blackberry smoothie.

1 cup marionberries, fresh or frozen

1 banana, fresh or frozen

1 to 1½ cups orange juice

1. Partially thaw the berries and banana, if frozen. Cut the banana into 3 or 4 pieces. Place the berries, banana, and 1 cup of the orange juice in a food processor or blender; process briefly. If not using fruit that was frozen, add a couple of ice cubes, then continue to process with intermittent pulses until all ingredients are blended. Add additional orange juice and process briefly until the desired texture is achieved. Pour into glasses and serve.

Cranberry-Raspberry Fruit Soup

BOREAS BED & BREAKFAST INN, LONG BEACH, WA

6 SERVINGS

This soup is a beautiful pink color and has some body to it, as some of the pulp will find its way through the sieve or food mill. It makes a delicious Valentine's soup—a sweet morning treat to bring a loved one for breakfast in bed. Serve it in chilled glass bowls, decorate with fresh berries, and top with a whipped cream heart!

1. In a 3-quart saucepan, bring the apple juice and cranberries to a boil. Reduce heat and simmer, uncovered, for 10 minutes. Add the raspberries; boil for a minute or two (if frozen). Press the fruit mixture through a sieve or run through a food mill to remove the seeds. Pour the juice back into the pan; bring to a boil. Add the sugar, lime juice, and cinnamon; stir until the sugar is dissolved. Remove from heat; let cool for 5 minutes.

2. In a small bowl, combine 1 cup of the fruit mixture with 1½ cups of the half-and-half. Stir back into the rest of the fruit mixture and bring to a gentle boil, stirring frequently. Whisk the cornstarch into the remaining half-and-half; stir into the soup. Cook and stir for 2 minutes (do not allow to come to a rolling boil); cool. Cover and refrigerate overnight.

3. Serve chilled soup in individual bowls. Top with berries and a dollop of whipped cream. Garnish with mint leaves.

2 cups apple juice

2 cups fresh or frozen cranberries

1 cup fresh or frozen raspberries

½ cup sugar

1 tablespoon freshly squeezed lime juice

½ teaspoon ground cinnamon

2 cups half-and-half, divided

1 tablespoon cornstarch

Fresh mixed berries

Whipped cream (optional)

Fresh mint leaves (optional)

Chardonnay-Poached Pears

INN ON ORCAS ISLAND, DEER HARBOR, WA

2 SERVINGS

These pears are incredibly delicious—they are perfectly tender, with just the right sweetness and a hint of chardonnay. They are simple to prepare, yet elegant to serve, and great with ice cream too! Use a small melon baller to easily core the pears.

¾ cup water

¼ cup chardonnay

½ cup sugar

1¼ teaspoons vanilla

2 Bosc pears, peeled, halved, and cored

4 ounces ricotta cheese

1. Combine the water, chardonnay, sugar, and vanilla in a small skillet or sauté pan; bring to a boil. Cover and simmer 8 minutes. Remove from heat and add the pear halves, cut side down. Cover and let cool to room temperature. Refrigerate overnight.

2. To serve, whip the ricotta in a small bowl; divide evenly between two stemmed glasses. Cube the pears and spoon over the ricotta. Spoon a tablespoon or two of poaching syrup over the pears.

Breakfast in Bed Made Simple

Coffee, tea, juice, champagne
Creamer, sugar cubes (with a small spoon to stir)
Warm croissants, muffins, toast, bagels
Jam, butter, cream cheese (with a small knife to spread)
Fresh berries or orange slices

"All happiness depends on a leisurely breakfast."
—JOHN GUNTHER

Granola with Honey Mascarpone

THE TUWANEK HOTEL, SECHELT, B.C.   **2 SERVINGS**

This recipe is a favorite with guests at the Tuwanek Hotel. The whipped cream topping takes the place of milk and makes for an elegant starter for two.

1. In a medium bowl, combine the granola, almonds, dates, cranberries, pear, and grapes.

2. Serve in individual bowls topped with a generous dollop of Honey Mascarpone. Garnish with mint leaves.

½ cup favorite granola

¼ cup slivered almonds, toasted

¼ cup chopped dates or dried apricots

2 tablespoons dried cranberries

½ ripe pear, diced

¼ cup chopped red grapes

Honey Mascarpone (recipe follows)

Fresh mint leaves (optional)

Honey Mascarpone

Lightly whip the cream in a small bowl. Add the honey and mascarpone cheese; continue whipping until creamy and smooth.

¼ cup whipping cream

1 tablespoon honey

1 tablespoon mascarpone cheese

Baked Apple Oatmeal

SELAH INN BED & BREAKFAST, BELFAIR, WA

9 SERVINGS

If you've never tasted baked oatmeal, you really need to try it. This is deliciously chewy, with just the right amount of sweetness. Make it on the weekend, and enjoy it throughout the week heated up in the microwave. You can also make it in individual ramekins—just reduce the baking time.

1. Preheat the oven to 350° F. Grease or spray an 8-inch-square baking pan with cooking spray. In a large mixing bowl, combine the sugar, oil, and eggs. Add the buttermilk, oatmeal, baking powder, salt, apples, and cranberries; mix well. Pour the mixture into the baking pan and bake until firm in the center, 35 to 40 minutes.

2. To serve, spoon the hot oatmeal into bowls, pour on half-and-half, and sprinkle with hazelnuts.

⅔ cup sugar

⅓ cup oil

2 eggs, beaten

3 cups buttermilk

3 cups old-fashioned oatmeal

2 teaspoons baking powder

1 teaspoon salt

1½ cups peeled, sliced baking apples

½ cup dried cranberries or cherries

Half-and-half or milk

Chopped toasted hazelnuts (optional)

Savory Swiss Scones

BROOKSIDE INN, CARLTON, OR **18 SCONES**

These scones are unique because they are round in shape and their texture is more like a baking powder biscuit—light and fluffy. Enjoy them warm with homemade jam.

1. Preheat the oven to 400°F. Grate the butter with the large-holed side of a cheese grater. In a large bowl, combine the flour, sugar, baking powder, baking soda, and salt with the butter; mix thoroughly. Add the sour cream and milk; mix until well combined. Turn the dough out on a floured work surface. Knead lightly, 3 or 4 turns.

2. Grease a cookie sheet. On a floured work surface, roll the dough into a 12- by 18-inch rectangle. Sprinkle the cheese evenly over the dough and gently press in. With the aid of a dough scraper, roll the dough into an 18-inch log. Cut into 1-inch slices. Place on the cookie sheet. Bake until the bottoms of the scones are golden brown, 15 to 20 minutes.

½ cup (1 stick) butter, frozen

2 cups flour

2 tablespoons sugar

1 tablespoon baking powder

¼ teaspoon baking soda

¾ teaspoon salt

½ cup sour cream

¼ cup whole milk or half-and-half

1 cup grated Gruyère or other Swiss cheese

Warm Scones with Apricot-Ginger Jam

8 SCONES

If you've only tried scones at the fair, don't be afraid to try making them yourself. You can make a double batch of the scone mix (up through adding the nuts) and refrigerate half of the mix for up to three weeks. The next time you want scones, just mix in the buttermilk, shape, and bake: you'll have warm-from-the-oven scones in fifteen minutes!

1. Preheat the oven to 400° F and grease a baking sheet. In a large bowl, stir together the flours, sugar, baking powder, baking soda, and salt. Using a pastry blender or two knives, cut the butter into the flour mixture until it resembles coarse crumbs. Stir in the nuts.

2. Make a well in the center of the flour mixture; add the buttermilk. Stir the mixture with a fork until the dough pulls away from the sides of the bowl. With your hands, gather the dough into a ball and place on a lightly floured board. Divide the dough into 2 parts and lightly pat each into a circle about ½ inch thick. Cut each circle into four equal wedges. Place the wedges on the greased baking sheet. Bake until golden brown, 14 to 16 minutes.

3. Serve warm with Apricot-Ginger Jam.

1 cup flour
½ cup whole wheat flour
¼ cup sugar
1¼ teaspoons baking powder
¼ teaspoon baking soda
½ teaspoon salt
6 tablespoons cold butter, cut into small pieces
½ cup chopped nuts (optional)
½ cup buttermilk
Apricot-Ginger Jam (recipe follows)

Apricot-Ginger Jam

Stir the preserves and fruit spread together until well combined.

⅓ cup ginger preserves
½ cup apricot fruit spread

Seven-in-One Buttermilk Scones

THE JAMES HOUSE, PORT TOWNSEND, WA

16 SCONES

Surprise your sweetie with a flavor-of-the-month scone! There are seven delicious variations to choose from. For convenience, you can even freeze the prebaked scones in foil and bake them frozen. Take out as many as you would like from the freezer, unwrap, and bake on a cookie sheet for 25 to 30 minutes.

1. Preheat the oven to 350°F. In a large bowl, mix the flour, sugar, baking powder, and salt. Cut the butter into the flour mixture with a pastry blender. Add the berries, tossing to coat. In a small bowl, beat the eggs with the buttermilk. Add the buttermilk mixture to flour mixture; stir until just combined.

2. Turn the dough out on a well-floured surface and knead lightly. (Note: If the dough is sticky, knead in a little more flour.) Divide in half and flatten into two circles, about 1 inch thick. Cut each circle into 8 wedges. Transfer to an ungreased baking sheet; let rest for 10 minutes. If desired, brush with half-and-half and sprinkle with sugar. Bake until golden brown, 15 to 20 minutes.

4½ cups all-purpose flour

1 cup sugar

2½ tablespoons baking powder

1½ teaspoons salt

½ cup (1 stick) cold butter, cut into pieces

1½ cups frozen blueberries or raspberries

3 eggs

1 cup plus 2 tablespoons buttermilk

Half-and-half (optional)

Sugar for sprinkling (optional)

Variations In place of the berries, substitute:

1½ cups chopped pecans; add 1 tablespoon pumpkin pie spice to dry ingredients

1½ cups chopped cranberries and 1 tablespoon orange zest

1 cup chopped walnuts and ½ cup grated coconut

1 cup chopped apple and ½ cup toffee chips

¾ cup dried cranberries and ¾ cup white chocolate chips

¼ cup poppy seeds and 1 tablespoon lemon zest

Pecan Pie Mini Muffins

CHANNEL HOUSE, DEPOE BAY, OR

2 DOZEN MINI MUFFINS

These sweet, chewy mini muffins are a perfect accompaniment to a shot of espresso in the morning. Even if you're not that fond of muffins, you'll be reaching for one more of these. Use roasted pecans in this recipe for a more intense nutty flavor.

1 cup chopped pecans

1 cup packed brown sugar

½ cup flour

⅔ cup butter, melted

2 eggs, beaten

Orange Cream Cheese Frosting (recipe follows)

1. Preheat the oven to 350° F. Grease or spray two mini muffin tins with cooking spray. In a large bowl, combine the pecans, brown sugar, and flour. Add the butter and eggs; stir until combined (batter will be shiny). Spoon a heaping tablespoon of batter into each mini muffin cup.

2. Bake for 20 minutes, or until a toothpick inserted in the center comes out clean. Let cool 5 minutes; transfer the muffins to a cooling rack.

3. To serve, spread a dollop of Orange Cream Cheese Frosting over each muffin.

Orange Cream Cheese Frosting

Whisk the cream cheese, butter, sugar, and orange zest together in a small bowl until creamy. For a stronger orange flavor, add a little more zest or a drop or two of orange extract.

¾ cup whipped cream cheese, at room temperature

1 tablespoon butter, at room temperature

½ cup powdered sugar

½ teaspoon orange zest

Orange extract (optional)

Magnificent Bran Muffins

HALFMOON BAY CABIN, HALFMOON BAY, B.C.

1 DOZEN MUFFINS

Your sweet tooth and health food craving can be satisfied at the same time with these muffins. For added crunch, substitute chopped walnuts for some of the dried fruit. To keep the muffins super-moist (and they are!), store them in a sealable plastic bag or an airtight container.

1. Preheat the oven to 350°F. Combine the dried fruit, raisins, baking soda, and boiling water in a medium bowl; let cool about 10 minutes. In a large bowl, mix the egg and brown sugar; stir in the oil, vanilla, and the dried fruit mixture. In a separate bowl, combine the flour, wheat bran, wheat germ, baking powder, and salt. Add the dry ingredients to the wet ingredients; stir just until combined.

2. Divide the batter evenly among 12 muffin cups. Bake until a toothpick inserted in the center comes out clean, 20 to 25 minutes (do not overbake).

1 cup chopped dried fruit (dates, apricots, peaches)

½ cup raisins or Craisins

1 teaspoon baking soda

1 cup boiling water

1 egg, beaten

¾ cup packed brown sugar

¼ cup vegetable oil

1½ teaspoons vanilla

1 cup whole wheat flour

½ cup wheat bran

¼ cup wheat germ or ground flaxseed

1 teaspoon baking powder

¼ teaspoon salt

Walnut and Black Pepper Biscotti

PATIT CREEK RESTAURANT, DAYTON, WA

2 DOZEN BISCOTTI

Biscotti are perfect for dunking into coffee (and dessert wine too). Be sure to allow time for the dough to chill for several hours and for the double baking that gives biscotti its special crunch. These will keep for up to one week if stored in an airtight container. If you prefer your biscotti a little sweeter, melt a little white chocolate and drizzle it over the biscotti with a fork.

1. In a large bowl, beat the butter. Add the sugar and continue beating until fluffy. Beat in the eggs, one at a time. Stir in the orange peel, vanilla, and almond extract. Mix in the walnuts. In a small bowl, combine the flour, baking soda, baking powder, pepper, and salt. Add the flour mixture to the butter-egg mixture; stir just until blended. Cover and refrigerate until well chilled, about 2 hours.

2. Preheat the oven to 350°F. Grease and flour a baking sheet. Using floured hands, divide the dough in half and form into two 3- by 9-inch rectangles on the baking sheet, leaving 3 inches in between. Bake for 20 minutes, or until a toothpick inserted in the center comes out clean. Cool on the baking sheet for 15 minutes, then transfer to a cutting board and cut the logs into ¾-inch slices, using a serrated knife. Arrange the slices, cut side down, on the baking sheet. Bake for 15 minutes, or until biscotti have reached desired crispness. Cool on a wire rack.

½ cup (1 stick) butter, softened

1 cup sugar

2 eggs

2 teaspoons grated orange peel

1½ teaspoons vanilla

½ teaspoon almond extract

1½ cups chopped walnuts, toasted

1¾ cups flour

½ teaspoon baking soda

½ teaspoon baking powder

1½ teaspoons freshly ground black pepper

⅛ teaspoon salt

Scottish Granola Bars

THE AERIE RESORT & SPA, MALAHAT, B.C. **48 BARS**

Packed full of wonderful good-for-you grains, nuts, and seeds, these bars will keep you going all day long. Wrap a couple up for you and your sweetie to enjoy with a midmorning cup of tea.

1. Preheat the oven to 350°F. Grease a jelly roll pan. In a large bowl, combine the oats, baking soda, flax and sesame seeds, millet, chocolate, and almonds. In a medium bowl, combine the butter, honey, corn syrup, and maple syrup. Add the liquid mixture to the dry ingredients. Add in the zests and stir until well combined.

2. Press the mixture into the greased pan. Bake for 20 minutes, or until golden brown. Let cool in the pan before cutting into bars.

1½ pounds Scottish oatmeal or 4¼ cups finely ground rolled oats

2 teaspoons baking soda

⅓ cup flaxseeds

⅔ cup sesame seeds

⅔ cup millet

1 cup (6 ounces) chopped dark chocolate

⅔ cup chopped almonds

¾ cup (1½ sticks) butter, melted

1 cup warm honey

⅓ cup corn syrup

⅓ cup maple syrup

Zest of 1 lemon

Zest of 1 orange

Ginger and Lemon Pear Pancakes

VILLA MARCO POLO INN, VICTORIA, B.C.

18 PANCAKES

*S*imply delicious! Tangy lemon peel with both fresh and crystallized ginger gives zing to these fabulous pear pancakes. For a special touch, garnish plates with edible flowers, like pansies or nasturtiums, or thin slices of pear that have been fanned out.

1. Mix the flour, baking powder, baking soda, and salt in a large bowl; set aside. In a medium bowl, beat the eggs at high speed until light and fluffy. Add the milk, brown sugar, and butter; continue beating until smooth. Stir in the pear, ginger, gingerroot, and lemon peel. Make a well in the center of the dry ingredients; add the wet ingredients and blend.

2. Preheat a griddle to 350°F or heat a skillet over medium-high heat. Brush the griddle or skillet with melted butter. Drop ¼-cup portions of batter onto the griddle. Cook until bubbles form on the surface, about 3 minutes. Turn and cook until golden on the other side.

3. To serve, place three pancakes on each plate, drizzle with Lemony Ginger Syrup, and add a dollop of whipped cream.

1½ cups flour

2 teaspoons baking powder

1 teaspoon baking soda

½ teaspoon salt

3 eggs

2 cups whole milk

¼ cup packed brown sugar

½ cup (1 stick) butter, melted

1½ red Anjou or Bartlett pears, coarsely grated

2 tablespoons finely chopped crystallized ginger

1 tablespoon grated gingerroot

1 teaspoon grated lemon peel

Melted butter for cooking

Lemony Ginger Syrup (recipe follows)

Whipped cream (optional)

Lemony Ginger Syrup

Put the sugar, corn syrup, and water in a small, heavy saucepan. Bring to a boil over medium heat. Lower heat and add the ginger. Simmer uncovered, stirring occasionally, until the mixture thickens slightly, 5 to 10 minutes. Add the lemon juice; simmer and allow the mixture to thicken again. Remove from heat and strain through a fine-mesh sieve. Store leftover syrup in the refrigerator for up to 1 week.

¾ cup sugar

¼ cup light corn syrup

¾ cup water

½ cup chopped peeled gingerroot

½ cup freshly squeezed lemon juice

Bubbly Waffles

MILLER TREE INN, FORKS, WA

8 SIX-INCH WAFFLES

You won't be able to resist these super-easy, super-yummy waffles, nor will anyone you're making them for. If you're feeling really decadent, use champagne in place of the soda, and then drink the rest with your orange juice.

1. In a large bowl, combine the pancake mix, egg, oil, and carbonated soda; stir until well blended. Pour the batter onto a hot waffle iron and cook until golden brown.

2. Serve warm with whipped cream and strawberries.

2 cups pancake or waffle mix

1 egg

½ cup vegetable oil

1⅓ cups clear carbonated soda (7-Up, club soda, seltzer)

Whipped cream (optional)

Fresh strawberries (optional)

Orange Croissant French Toast

2 SERVINGS

You'll find this recipe is even better using day-old croissants—a perfect reason to buy a couple of extra while at the bakery!

1. In a small, shallow bowl, combine the eggs and orange juice and zest. Heat the butter in a medium skillet over medium-low heat. Dip the croissant halves in the egg mixture and cook until golden brown on both sides. Sprinkle with powdered sugar. Serve with berries and maple syrup.

2 eggs, beaten

2 tablespoons freshly squeezed orange juice

½ teaspoon orange zest

2 to 3 teaspoons butter, melted

2 croissants, cut in half horizontally

Powdered sugar (optional)

Fresh berries (optional)

Maple syrup

Baked Blueberry-Pecan French Toast

AUTUMN LEAVES BED AND BREAKFAST, ANACORTES, WA

6 SERVINGS

Ease your morning by prepping this dish the night before. In the morning, pop it in the oven with some foil-wrapped ham (lightly sprinkled with maple syrup). This is a perfect way to celebrate fresh blueberries when they're in season.

1. Grease or spray a 9- by 13-inch baking pan with cooking spray. Cut the baguette into twelve 1-inch slices; remove any hard crusts. Arrange the slices in a single layer in the pan. Whisk together the eggs, milk, vanilla, and nutmeg in a medium bowl. Pour over the bread, making sure the slices are saturated from top to bottom. Cover and refrigerate for at least 4 hours or overnight.

2. Heat the oven to 350° F. Sprinkle the pecans and blueberries evenly over the bread. Cut the butter into pieces and add to the brown sugar in a microwave-safe container. Microwave until melted, stirring occasionally. (Alternatively, cut the butter into pieces and melt in a small saucepan over medium-low heat; add the brown sugar and stir until combined.) Drizzle the mixture over the bread. Bake until the liquid from the blueberries is bubbling, 35 to 40 minutes. Serve with maple syrup.

1 baguette

6 eggs

1½ cups milk

1 teaspoon vanilla

½ teaspoon ground nutmeg

1 cup pecans

2 cups blueberries, fresh or frozen (not thawed)

4 tablespoons (½ stick) butter

¼ cup packed brown sugar

Maple syrup (optional)

Dreamy Brûlée French Toast

THE DREAMGIVER'S INN, NEWBERG, OR

6 SERVINGS

This is a very simple yet elegant breakfast dish. It's sweet and wonderful just as it is, or you can top it with fresh berries or caramelized pears. This is perfect served with apple chicken sausage or pepper bacon. Leftovers reheat nicely in the microwave or in the oven at a low temperature.

1. In a small, heavy saucepan, melt the butter over medium heat. Add the brown sugar and corn syrup and stir until smooth. Pour into a 9- by 13-inch baking dish. Cut six 1-inch-thick slices from the center of the bread loaf. Arrange the bread slices in one layer in the baking dish, squeezing them slightly to fit.

2. In a medium bowl, whisk together the eggs, half-and-half, vanilla, Grand Marnier, and salt until well combined; pour evenly over the bread. Cover and chill at least 8 hours and up to 1 day.

3. Bring the bread to room temperature. Preheat the oven to 350°F. Bake, uncovered, in the middle of the oven until the French toast is puffed and the edges are light golden brown, 35 to 40 minutes. Serve immediately.

½ cup (1 stick) butter

1 cup packed brown sugar

2 tablespoons corn syrup

1 loaf French or Tuscan-style bread

5 eggs

1½ cups half-and-half

1 teaspoon vanilla

1 teaspoon Grand Marnier or orange zest

¼ teaspoon salt

Cheese Blintz Soufflé with Warm Blueberry Sauce

A COWSLIP'S BELLE BED & BREAKFAST, ASHLAND, OR   **8 SERVINGS**

This soufflé is sweet and elegant when served in individual dishes with the warm blueberry sauce drizzled over it. It tastes a bit like a not-so-sweet cheesecake—a wonderful morning indulgence for two!

1. Preheat the oven to 350°F. Grease or spray a 9- by 13-inch baking dish with cooking spray. In a large bowl, cream the butter and sugar together. Add the eggs; beat well. In a small bowl, combine the flour and baking powder. In another small bowl, mix the yogurt and orange juice. Add the flour mixture alternately with the yogurt mixture to the egg mixture; stir until just combined. Pour half of the batter into the prepared baking dish.

2. For the filling, in a small bowl, beat the cream cheese until smooth. Add the ricotta, egg yolks, sugar, and vanilla; mix thoroughly (it will be thick). Carefully spread the filling over the batter. Pour the remaining batter over the filling. Bake for 50 minutes, or until golden brown. Serve warm with a drizzle of Warm Blueberry Sauce.

½ cup (1 stick) butter, softened

⅓ cup sugar

6 eggs

1 cup flour

2 tablespoons baking powder

1½ cups plain yogurt

½ cup orange juice

One 8-ounce package cream cheese

One 15-ounce container ricotta cheese

2 egg yolks

1 tablespoon sugar

1 teaspoon vanilla

Warm Blueberry Sauce (recipe follows)

Warm Blueberry Sauce

Whisk together the water, sugar, and flour in a small saucepan. Cook over medium heat until thickened. Add the blueberries. If using fresh berries, cook for 1 minute; if using frozen, cook until completely thawed, stirring occasionally. Remove the pan from the heat. Add the butter and cinnamon; stir until the butter is melted. Serve warm.

1 cup water

¼ cup sugar

1 tablespoon flour

1 cup fresh or frozen blueberries

½ tablespoon butter

¼ teaspoon ground cinnamon

Feta, Basil, and Tomato Pie

SALISBURY HOUSE, SEATTLE, WA

6 SERVINGS

The first tomatoes grown in Europe were called *pommes d'amour*, or "love apples," as they were believed to have aphrodisiacal powers. Use garden tomatoes when they're in season and fresh basil whenever it's available.

1. Preheat the oven to 375° F. Place the piecrust in a 9-inch glass pie plate; crimp edges if desired. Bake crust until light golden brown, 7 to 9 minutes. Remove from the oven. Sprinkle the feta in the bottom of the warm piecrust. Top with the tomatoes, basil, and Monterey Jack cheese.

2. Whisk together the eggs, milk, and half-and-half in a small bowl; pour over the cheese. Bake for 30 minutes, or until pie is set in the middle. (Note: You may need to use a piecrust ring or wrap aluminum foil around the piecrust edge to prevent overbrowning.) Let cool 5 to 10 minutes before cutting. Garnish with a fresh basil leaf on each slice. Serve warm.

1 refrigerated piecrust or savory pastry dough

1 cup crumbled feta cheese

3 plum tomatoes, thinly sliced

⅓ cup chopped fresh basil leaves or 2 teaspoons dried basil

½ cup shredded Monterey Jack cheese

4 eggs

⅓ cup milk

⅓ cup half-and-half

Fresh basil leaves (optional)

Chicken and Asparagus Crepes

ENGLISH BAY INN, VANCOUVER, B.C.   **16 CREPES**

Crepes are special because they're not something you make very often. Prepare these when you want to treat your friends and loved ones to a special brunch. Much of the preparation for these can be done ahead of time; in fact, the crepe batter must be refrigerated for at least an hour before cooking.

1. Prepare the crepes; set aside. Steam the asparagus and green onions until crisp-tender, about 5 minutes.

2. Heat the butter in a 10-inch nonstick skillet over medium heat. Add the chicken, parsley, and tarragon and cook just until the chicken begins to brown.

3. In a large bowl, cream together the cheeses; add the egg and stir until well combined. Stir in the chicken and asparagus.

4. To assemble the crepes, preheat the oven to 350°F. Spoon ½ cup of the filling down the center of each crepe and fold in the sides, overlapping the filling. Place the crepes, folded side up, in a single layer in two 7- by 11-inch baking pans. Cover the pans with aluminum foil and bake until hot, 15 to 20 minutes. Serve warm.

16 Basic Crepes (recipe follows)

1 pound fresh asparagus spears, cut in 1-inch pieces

1 bunch green onions (white and pale green parts), chopped

½ tablespoon butter

1 pound chicken breasts, cut into 1½- by ½-inch strips

2 tablespoons minced fresh parsley

2½ teaspoons dried tarragon or Italian seasoning

1 pound (16 ounces) cream cheese, at room temperature

½ cup grated Parmesan cheese

½ cup shredded Swiss cheese

1 egg, well beaten

Basic Crepes

In a medium bowl, beat the eggs; beat in the milk and water. Gradually whisk in the flour and salt. Add the melted butter and stir until smooth. Cover and refrigerate for at least one hour and up to 24 hours. Heat a 10-inch nonstick crepe pan over medium heat until hot. Coat the pan lightly with butter and pour in ¼ cup of the crepe batter, rotating the pan to coat the bottom. Cook until almost dry at the top and slightly browned on the edges. Loosen the edges with a spatula and flip the crepe over. Cook the other side until slightly browned. Turn the crepe out onto a flat plate to cool. Repeat with the remaining mixture. Stack the crepes as they are cooked. (Note: Crepes can be wrapped with plastic wrap at this point and refrigerated for up to 3 days.)

4 eggs

2 cups milk

⅔ cup water

2 cups flour

½ teaspoon salt

¼ cup (½ stick) butter, melted

Butter for cooking

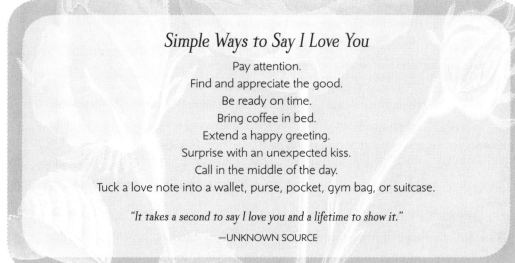

Simple Ways to Say I Love You

Pay attention.
Find and appreciate the good.
Be ready on time.
Bring coffee in bed.
Extend a happy greeting.
Surprise with an unexpected kiss.
Call in the middle of the day.
Tuck a love note into a wallet, purse, pocket, gym bag, or suitcase.

"It takes a second to say I love you and a lifetime to show it."

—UNKNOWN SOURCE

Oregon Dungeness Crab Quiche

PINE RIDGE INN, BEND, OR

6 TO 8 SERVINGS

Serve this with fresh fruit and muffins for breakfast or with Pears with Goat Cheese, Pine Nuts, and Honey (page 51) for a light dinner. Bonus—this quiche is even more delicious when reheated.

1. Preheat the oven to 400° F. Place the piecrust in a 9-inch quiche dish, pressing the dough down firmly with your fingers. Press the Parmesan cheese and dill weed into the crust. Prick the bottoms and sides of the dough with a fork. Line the crust with parchment paper and fill it with pie weights or dried beans. Bake for 10 minutes. Remove the weights; return the crust to the oven for 3 minutes to brown slightly.

2. Steam the asparagus stems until crisp-tender. Cut off the tips with 2 inches of stem and reserve; chop the stems. Combine the Jarlsberg and Emmentaler cheeses and sprinkle half over the bottom of the crust. Top with the crabmeat (reserve the claw meat), chopped asparagus stems, and remaining cheese. In a small bowl, whisk together the half-and-half, eggs, horseradish, Tabasco, crab cake seasoning, white pepper, and salt. Pour the egg mixture carefully over the cheese, gently separating the cheese with a fork and allowing the liquid to penetrate. Arrange the claw meat alternately with the reserved asparagus tips to form a spoke pattern on top. Sprinkle with a couple of dashes of nutmeg, crab cake seasoning, and, if you like, more dill weed.

3. Bake until the pie is set and light golden brown, 35 to 40 minutes. (Note: You may need to use a piecrust ring or wrap aluminum foil around the piecrust edge to prevent overbrowning.) Cool 10 to 15 minutes before cutting. (To reheat for serving later, bake for 25 to 30 minutes at 325° F.) The baked pie will keep, refrigerated, for up to 2 days.

1 refrigerated piecrust or savory pastry dough

1 tablespoon grated Parmesan cheese

½ teaspoon dried dill weed

8 slender stems asparagus

¾ cup Jarlsberg cheese

¾ cup Emmentaler cheese

1 pound Dungeness crabmeat with claw meat

1¼ cups half-and-half

4 eggs

1 tablespoon prepared horseradish

3 generous dashes Tabasco sauce

½ teaspoon Tom Douglas "Rub with Love" Crab Cake Seasoning or ground chipotle powder

¼ teaspoon white pepper

⅛ teaspoon salt

Freshly ground nutmeg

Baked Eggs with Gruyère, Tarragon, and Leeks

LIGHTHOUSE BED AND BREAKFAST, BANDON, OR   **8 SERVINGS**

Here's a tasty dish that can be made the night before. Leeks are related to onions and garlic (they look like a giant green onion), but their flavor is subtler. Leeks can be dirty, so wash them well by cutting them lengthwise, then rinsing them in water.

1. Preheat the oven to 375° F. Grease or spray a 9- by 13-inch baking dish with cooking spray. In small skillet, heat the butter over medium heat; add the leeks and sauté until tender. Spread the leeks in the bottom of the baking dish. In a small bowl, combine the cheeses; spread all but ½ cup over the leeks. In a medium bowl, whisk the eggs, half-and-half, tarragon, and pepper; pour over the cheese. (Note: At this point the dish can be covered and refrigerated overnight. Remove from the refrigerator 15 minutes before baking.)

2. Bake until the top is golden brown and the center is set, 30 to 35 minutes. Sprinkle with the remaining cheese; return to the oven until the cheese melts.

3 tablespoons butter

3 to 4 large leeks (white and pale green parts only), coarsely chopped

1½ cups shredded Gruyère or other Swiss cheese

½ cup grated Parmesan cheese

8 eggs

2 cups half-and-half

3 tablespoons fresh tarragon leaves or 1 teaspoon dried tarragon

Freshly ground black pepper

Asparagus Frittata

EAGLE ROCK LODGE, VIDA, OR

4 TO 6 SERVINGS

For a special touch, serve this frittata with a dollop of sour cream or roasted red bell pepper sauce (available in jars at specialty markets). Frittatas are great for using up leftover veggies or meat, and any hard cheese you have on hand will be fine.

1. In a medium skillet (with an ovenproof handle), heat the oil and butter over medium heat. Add the onions, asparagus, and garlic; cook until the onions begin to caramelize and the asparagus is tender, 8 to 12 minutes (depending on the thickness).

2. Preheat the broiler. In a small bowl, beat the eggs, water, and salt. Pour the egg mixture into the skillet with the vegetables; stir in the Swiss cheese. Cover and cook until the eggs are almost set but still runny on top, 2 to 3 minutes. Put the skillet in the oven and broil until light golden brown, about 45 seconds. (Note: Watch this carefully, as the top can burn easily). Sprinkle with Parmesan cheese before serving.

1 tablespoon olive oil

2 tablespoons butter

½ cup thinly sliced Walla Walla or other sweet onion

1 cup chopped fresh asparagus

2 cloves garlic, minced

6 eggs

1 tablespoon water

¼ teaspoon salt

½ cup grated Swiss cheese

Parmesan cheese (optional)

Mom's Cheddar Baked Eggs

SALT SPRING VINEYARDS BED AND BREAKFAST, SALT SPRING ISLAND, B.C.

2 SERVINGS

This recipe is called Mom's because it was handed down from the innkeeper's mother. The innkeeper says, "It looked so simple when she gave it to me that I figured it couldn't taste that exciting. One day I was running short of prep time and tried it, and I have been serving it ever since."

1. Preheat the oven to 350° F. Grease or spray two 3-inch ramekins with cooking spray. Place 1 teaspoon of butter in each ramekin; top with 2 tablespoons of the grated cheese. Crack 1 egg into each dish, being careful not to break the yolk.

2. In a small bowl, combine the half-and-half and mustard; whisk until well combined. Pour 1 tablespoon over each egg. Bake for 15 minutes. Sprinkle with the remaining cheese and continue baking for 3 minutes, or until the whites are set and the cheese is melted. Season to taste with pepper.

2 teaspoons melted butter, divided

⅓ cup grated cheddar cheese, divided

2 eggs

2 tablespoons half-and-half

¼ teaspoon dry mustard

Freshly ground black pepper (optional)

Lox Benedict with Lemon-Caper Sauce

LOST MOUNTAIN LODGE, SEQUIM, WA

2 SERVINGS

When it comes to breakfast, this is as special as it gets! Each bite is an explosion of wonderful tastes, flavors, and textures. This can be fun to prepare with or for your special someone; the steps are not so difficult—and well worth the effort!

1. To make the Lemon-Caper Sauce, whisk the broth and cornstarch together in a small saucepan until smooth. Stir over medium-high heat until it boils, 2 to 3 minutes. Reduce heat to medium-low, then whisk in the sour cream, lemon juice, capers, and salt. Stir frequently until heated, about 2 minutes. Do not let mixture boil. Season to taste with pepper. Keep warm over very low heat until ready to serve.

2. To make the Lox Benedict, in a small skillet, heat the olive oil and butter over medium heat until the butter is melted. Add the garlic and cook until golden brown, 1 to 2 minutes. Add the spinach and cook until slightly wilted; set aside.

3. Poach the eggs: Heat 2 inches of water to boiling in a medium skillet; reduce to simmering. Break each egg into a custard cup and then carefully slip into the water one egg at a time. Cook until the egg whites and yolks are firm but not runny, 3 to 5 minutes. Remove with a slotted spoon to a paper towel.

4. To assemble, place two English muffin halves on each plate; top with sautéed spinach and lox. Gently slide a poached egg on top of each. Ladle warm Lemon-Caper Sauce over the top.

⅔ cup vegetable or chicken broth

1 tablespoon cornstarch

½ cup reduced-fat sour cream

1 tablespoon freshly squeezed lemon juice

2 tablespoons capers, well drained

⅛ teaspoon salt

Freshly ground black pepper

½ tablespoon olive oil

½ tablespoon butter

½ teaspoon minced garlic

4 cups fresh baby spinach

4 eggs

2 multigrain English muffins, split and toasted lightly

4 ounces cold-smoked salmon lox

Pesto Breakfast Quesadillas

MORGAN HILL RETREAT, POULSBO, WA

2 SERVINGS

For those of you not interested in a leisurely breakfast, these quesadillas are incredibly simple—they can practically be eaten on the run. If you make your own pesto in the summer, freeze it in ice cube trays to use all year round.

Four 7-inch flour tortillas

2 tablespoons pesto (more or less)

2 tablespoons cream cheese (more or less)

3 to 4 eggs, scrambled until set but still moist

Tomato slices (optional)

Avocado slices (optional)

1. Warm a griddle or skillet over medium heat. Spread two tortillas with pesto and two tortillas with cream cheese. Put the pesto-spread tortillas, pesto side up, on the griddle; top with the eggs. Place the cream cheese–spread tortilla over the eggs, creating a sandwich; cook until golden brown, about 1 minute. Carefully flip the quesadilla and cook for another minute. (For crisper tortillas, heat longer on each side.)

2. To serve, cut into quarters and serve garnished with tomato and avocado slices.

Fun Ways with Champagne

Make mimosas with fresh tangerine juice.

Use in risotto in place of white wine.

Make Bubbly Waffles (page 16).

Mix with sugar and use as an exfoliant.

Drink with floating pomegranate seeds.

Mix with an ounce of cassis for a Kir Royale.

Create a Black Velvet (equal parts Guinness and champagne).

Enjoy with fresh or smoked oysters.

Sip or splash in a bath for two.

Soak a sugar cube with Angostura bitters and place in the bottom of a champagne flute—fill with champagne for a classic cocktail.

"There comes a time in every woman's life when the only thing that helps is a glass of champagne."

—BETTE DAVIS

Appetizers & Small Plates

Amazing Dates	*Bookwalter Winery*
Broiled Portobello Mushrooms	*Tucker House*
Balsamic Mushrooms and Brie Toast	*Beaconsfield Inn*
Fried Brie with Green Onions	*Dunham Cellars*
Sweet Pepper Tapenade Toasts	*Lara House Lodge*
Shrimp Crostini	*Ann Starrett Mansion*
Scallops à la Parmesana	*Andina Restaurant*
Fresh Oysters with Tabasco and Lemongrass Granité	*Point No Point Resort*
Roasted Westcott Bay Oysters with Hazelnut-Garlic-Basil Butter	*The Place Bar & Grill*
Sizzling Mussels	*T's Restaurant*
Steamed Clams in Saffron Broth	*Mona's Bistro and Lounge*

Amazing Dates

BOOKWALTER WINERY, RICHLAND, WA

2 OR MORE SERVINGS

Spend less time cooking and more time together! You can easily make these for a large group or prepare just enough for two. These are intensely rich and sensual, so it's best to use the smaller dates (found in the grocery store's dried fruit section), rather than the larger Medjool dates (found in the produce department).

Whole dried dates, pitted

Raw or smoked whole almonds

Apple-smoked bacon slices (not thick-sliced)

1. Preheat the oven to 350°F. Stuff each date with 1 or 2 almonds (depending on size of date). Cut the bacon in half or in thirds; wrap each date with a piece of bacon and place it seam side down on a foil-lined baking pan with sides (such as a jelly roll pan).

2. Bake until the bacon is just beginning to brown and crisp, about 25 minutes. Serve hot.

Broiled Portobello Mushrooms

TUCKER HOUSE, FRIDAY HARBOR, WA

1 DOZEN MUSHROOMS

These are lip-smackingly delicious served hot out of the oven. They are luscious and juicy, so make sure you have cocktail napkins handy. To make soft bread crumbs, lightly toast two pieces of bread and pulse in a food processor.

1. Preheat the broiler. To make the filling, remove the mushroom stems and finely chop them. In a medium skillet, heat 1 tablespoon of the butter; add the onion and mushroom stems and cook for about 2 minutes, or until the onion is translucent. Mix in the bread crumbs, sausage, oregano, and enough sherry to moisten the mixture. Season with salt and pepper.

2. In a small saucepan, melt the remaining butter. Place the mushroom caps on a baking sheet, stem side down. Brush the tops with 1 table-spoon of the melted butter; broil for 2 minutes. Turn the caps over and brush the stem sides with the remaining melted butter.

3. Fill each mushroom cap with a heaping teaspoon of the filling. Broil until hot, about 3 minutes. Serve warm.

12 large baby portobello mushrooms (about 2 inches in diameter)

3 tablespoons butter, divided

1 small yellow onion, finely chopped

1 cup fine soft bread crumbs

½ cup finely chopped precooked Italian or apple sausage

½ teaspoon crumbled dried oregano leaves

2 to 3 tablespoons sherry or white wine

Salt and freshly ground pepper to taste

Balsamic Mushrooms and Brie Toast

BEACONSFIELD INN, VICTORIA, B.C.   **6 SERVINGS**

This is a wonderful recipe to prepare in the fall, when the variety of mushrooms is at its best. Choose plump, meaty ones that hold their texture when cooked, such as portobello and shiitake. Mix them up for contrast in flavor and texture. Topping them with a thick slice of creamy Brie that just starts to melt from the heat of the sauce makes this dish quite special!

1. Heat the olive oil and butter in a sauté pan over medium heat, until the butter starts to foam; add the rosemary and mushrooms. Stir occasionally until the mushrooms start to soften, 2 to 3 minutes. Add the vinegar, salt, and pepper. Reduce the vinegar over high heat until it turns syrupy, 7 to 8 minutes. Add the cream and continue cooking on high heat so the cream boils and reduces, 2 to 3 minutes. When the liquid in the pan is thickened and glossy, remove from heat. Discard the rosemary sprigs.

2. To serve, toast the bread, butter generously, and place on individual plates. Spoon the mushroom sauce over the toast, using all the sauce (the bread will soak it up). Place a slice of Brie and a fresh sprig of rosemary on top of each portion and serve immediately.

¼ cup light olive oil

4 tablespoons butter, plus additional for buttering toast

2 sprigs fresh rosemary

4 cups sliced mushrooms, any variety

⅓ cup good-quality balsamic vinegar

½ teaspoon salt

¼ teaspoon freshly ground black pepper

⅔ cup whipping cream

6 thick slices good-quality whole grain or sourdough bread

6 thick slices (about 6 ounces) triple-cream Brie, at room temperature

6 small sprigs fresh rosemary

Fried Brie with Green Onions

DUNHAM CELLARS, WALLA WALLA, WA

8 SERVINGS

Delicious! Serve this rich and gooey Brie with French bread or assorted crackers and fresh fruit. It's also quite delicious served with a sweet condiment such as Blackberry Balsamic Gastrique (page 99), jalapeño jelly, or your favorite chutney.

1. In a small shallow dish, beat the egg well. Put the bread crumbs in a separate shallow dish. Dip the cheese round first in the egg, then in the bread crumbs, turning several times to coat evenly. Refrigerate the coated cheese, uncovered, for 30 minutes.

2. To fry, heat 2 tablespoons of the butter over medium heat in a small skillet. Fry the cheese in the butter until the bottom is golden brown, 4 to 5 minutes. Turn over, cover, and continue cooking until the other side is golden brown and the cheese is warmed through, about 2 minutes. Meanwhile, sauté the green onions in the remaining butter.

3. To serve, place the cheese on a platter and sprinkle with the green onions.

1 egg

Italian dry bread crumbs

1 small (8 ounces) round Brie cheese

3 tablespoons butter, divided

3 green onions (white and green parts), chopped

Sweet Pepper Tapenade Toasts

LARA HOUSE LODGE, BEND, OR

24 TOASTS

Peppadews are delicious pickled sweet and piquant red peppers imported from South Africa. You can purchase them in a jar (in the condiments section), or if you have a good deli or olive bar in your area you will often find them there. This recipe combines Peppadews with capers and feta to make a wonderful topping for baguette toasts.

1. Preheat the oven to 375°F. Place the baguette rounds on a baking sheet; brush both sides with olive oil. Toast the rounds in the oven until lightly browned, 12 to 14 minutes, turning them halfway through. Rub the toasts with the garlic and set aside.

2. In a medium bowl, stir together the Peppadews, capers, oil, feta, basil, and pepper until well combined. To serve, top garlic toasts with a small amount of Peppadew tapenade.

1 baguette, sliced into ¼-inch rounds

Olive oil

1 garlic clove, peeled and halved

1 cup drained, diced Peppadews

⅓ cup drained capers

⅓ cup olive oil

1 cup crumbled feta cheese

¼ cup chopped fresh basil leaves

Freshly cracked black pepper

Shrimp Crostini

18 CROSTINI

This is a super-quick appetizer, perfect for last-minute company. The best part is that it looks like you've gone to a lot of work when really you haven't. (In a pinch, you can even use canned baby shrimp.) The Meyer lemon is a bit sweeter than a regular lemon (it is a cross between a lemon and a mandarin orange) and is available November through April.

1 baguette, sliced into ¼-inch rounds

Olive oil

½ pound fresh or frozen small peeled cooked shrimp

⅓ cup mayonnaise

Freshly squeezed juice of 1 Meyer or regular lemon

2 tablespoons chopped fresh parsley or dill

Freshly cracked black pepper

Snipped fresh chives or chopped parsley

1. Preheat the oven to 400° F. Brush both sides of the baguette rounds with olive oil and place on a baking sheet. Bake until golden brown, 8 to 10 minutes.

2. If using frozen shrimp, thaw by rinsing them in a colander; pat dry with a paper towel. In a small bowl, combine the mayonnaise and lemon juice. Fold in the shrimp and parsley. Season to taste with pepper.

3. To serve, place a heaping tablespoon of the shrimp mixture on each crostini. Garnish with chives. Serve immediately.

Scallops à la Parmesana

ANDINA RESTAURANT, PORTLAND, OR

2 SERVINGS

These tender morsels are simple to prepare and exquisite on the lips. Succulent bay scallops are kissed with citrus, encrusted with Parmesan, and then lightly glazed with shallots and butter. Broil in scrubbed scallop shells for an even more impressive presentation.

1. Preheat the broiler. Combine the scallops with the lime juice, and season with salt and pepper; divide evenly between two 6-ounce ramekins. Sprinkle each ramekin with half of the cheese; top with half of the Shallot Butter. Broil just until cheese turns golden brown (watch closely), about 1 to 2 minutes. Serve with lime wedges.

8 ounces bay scallops

2 tablespoons Key lime juice

Salt and freshly ground black pepper

⅓ cup shredded Parmesan cheese, divided

1 tablespoon Shallot Butter (recipe follows), softened, divided

Lime wedges

Shallot Butter

In a food processor, blend the butter and shallot until smooth. (Note: Place any leftover butter in an airtight container and refrigerate for up to 2 weeks.)

½ cup (1 stick) butter

1 medium shallot, diced

Fresh Oysters with Tabasco and Lemongrass Granité

POINT NO POINT RESORT, SOOKE, B.C.

2 SERVINGS

Granité (or granita) is simple to make and elegant to serve. It can be sweet, savory, peppery hot, refreshingly tart, or anything else you want it to be. It has a coarse, crystalline texture, much like that of a snow cone. This granité has a little kick to it and is served as a refreshing complement to fresh oysters.

1. To make the granité, bruise the lemongrass stalks with a saucepan or a meat tenderizer. Place the ginger ale, lemon juice, gingerroot, Tabasco, and peppercorns in a medium saucepan and bring to a boil. Simmer for 5 minutes and strain. Add the vodka. Pour a thin layer onto a 9- by 13-inch baking sheet and freeze for 4 hours or overnight. When frozen, transfer chunks to a food processor and pulse until slushy. Refreeze for several hours until frozen.

2. When ready to serve, shuck the oysters, making sure to cut off the bottom muscle; place them back on the half shell. Use a fork to scrape the granité down the length of the pan, forming icy flakes. Place the granité in a small chilled glass bowl and serve alongside the oysters on the half shell.

2 stalks fresh lemongrass

2 cups ginger ale

⅓ cup freshly squeezed lemon juice

1-inch piece gingerroot, peeled and diced

1 or 2 dashes Tabasco sauce

10 black peppercorns

¼ cup vodka

1 dozen chilled Miyagi, Pacific, or other fresh oysters

Roasted Westcott Bay Oysters with Hazelnut-Garlic-Basil Butter

THE PLACE BAR & GRILL, FRIDAY HARBOR, WA

2 SERVINGS

You just can't go wrong with roasting oysters. If you have leftover Hazelnut-Garlic-Basil Butter, it is fabulous on grilled or oven-braised fish, as well as on chicken and pork.

1. Preheat the oven to 475° F. Shuck the oysters, making sure to cut off the bottom muscle; place them back on the half shell. Place a layer of coarse salt in the bottom of a small baking dish. Place the oysters on top of the salt (the salt keeps the oysters upright).

2. Place a scant teaspoonful of the Hazelnut-Garlic-Basil Butter on top of each oyster; bake until the butter just begins to bubble and turn a light golden brown, about 10 minutes.

3. Serve the oysters on a platter with lemon wedges, on a bed of salad greens or on fresh coarse salt (again, this keeps the oysters upright so the butter doesn't spill out).

12 to 18 oysters in the shell

Coarse salt, for presentation

Hazelnut-Garlic-Basil Butter (recipe follows)

Lemon wedges (optional)

Fresh salad greens (optional)

Hazelnut-Garlic-Basil Butter

Preheat the oven to 400° F. Spread the nuts on a sheet pan and bake for 10 minutes. Roll in a kitchen towel to remove the skins. Chop the toasted nuts in a food processor until fine, but not ground. Add the butter and process until well blended. Add the lemon juice, garlic, basil, Parmesan, and Pernod; process well, scraping down the sides of the bowl to fully incorporate all the ingredients. (Note: Place any leftover butter in an airtight container and refrigerate for up to 2 weeks.)

¼ cup raw hazelnuts

½ cup butter, at room temperature

1 teaspoon freshly squeezed lemon juice

1 clove garlic, minced

½ tablespoon chopped fresh basil

¼ cup grated Parmesan or other hard Italian cheese

½ teaspoon Pernod, ouzo, or sambuca, or 2 drops anise extract

Sizzling Mussels

T'S RESTAURANT, PORT TOWNSEND, WA

2 SERVINGS

Nothing says Northwest more than a bowl of fresh steamed mussels and an ice-cold microbrew. These make a buttery garlic broth for succulent bread dipping. And the mussels really do sizzle!

1. In a medium skillet, heat the olive oil over medium heat. Add the shallot and garlic; sauté until the shallot is translucent, about 3 minutes. Add the herb sprigs and the mussels; cook for 1 minute. Add the wine; cook until the mussels open, about 5 minutes. Discard any that do not open. Stir in the butter and season with salt and pepper. Serve immediately with bread for dipping.

1 tablespoon olive oil

1 shallot, minced

3 garlic cloves, minced

1 sprig fresh rosemary

1 sprig fresh tarragon

1 sprig fresh thyme

1 pound mussels, scrubbed and debearded

½ cup white wine

3 tablespoons butter

Salt and freshly ground black pepper

Warm crusty bread

Steamed Clams in Saffron Broth

MONA'S BISTRO AND LOUNGE, SEATTLE, WA   **2 SERVINGS**

Though saffron is the world's most expensive spice, don't let that scare you off. Surely you and your love are worth it. The Saffron Vin will last for months and can be used for several batches of steamed clams. Make sure you have some good bread (it's great grilled) to soak up every drop of the delicious broth.

1. Scrub the clams with a vegetable brush in cold water. Heat a large sauté pan. Add the oil and sauté the garlic and shallots over medium heat until the shallots are transparent, about 3 minutes. Add the clams. Deglaze the pan with the wine. Add the stock; cover and let the clams steam until all are open, about 2 minutes. Discard any that do not open. Stir in the tomatoes and Saffron Vin. Season to taste with salt and pepper.

2. To serve, transfer to a serving dish. Sprinkle with parsley.

Note: To remove any sand, put the clams in a gallon of water and add ⅓ cup kosher salt and 1 cup cornmeal. Let them sit for 1 hour.

2½ pounds steamer clams (see Note)

1½ tablespoons olive oil

1 clove garlic, sliced

1 shallot, diced

2 to 3 tablespoons white wine

½ cup fish or vegetable stock

¼ cup sun-dried tomatoes packed in oil

2 tablespoons Saffron Vin (recipe follows)

Salt and freshly ground black pepper

1 tablespoon finely chopped fresh parsley

Saffron Vin

Heat the sherry in a heavy small saucepan over medium heat until reduced to one third of its original volume, 8 to 10 minutes. Remove from heat and add the saffron (the sherry will turn bright red). Let rest for 5 minutes. Whisk in the sugar. Whisk in the oil slowly until blended. Store in an airtight jar or bottle in a cool, dark place.

½ cup sherry

¼ teaspoon saffron

½ teaspoon sugar

⅓ cup light olive oil

Perfect Pairs

Cheeses to sample and wines to share

Cheese	Serve with	Pair with
Cambozola (Germany)	Crostini and roasted garlic	Syrah/Shiraz
Humbolt Fog (California)	Black mission figs and honey	Pinot grigio or prosecco
Gjetost (Norway)	Crispbread and green apple	Port or late-harvest white
Morbier (France)	French bread and chutney	Syrah/Shiraz
Jarlsberg (Norway)	Sausages, crackers, mustard	Riesling
Smoked mozzarella (USA)	Honeycrisp apples	Big, buttery, oaky chardonnay
Manchego (Spain)	Crusty bread and quince paste	Rioja or tempranillo
Parmigiano-Reggiano (Italy)	Grapes and walnuts	Barbera or Montepulciano
Goat Gouda (Holland)	Ripe pear wedges	Gewürztraminer or petite sirah
Barrel-aged feta (Greece)	Assorted olives and peppers	Chardonnay, gewürztraminer

"Bachelor's fare: Bread, cheese, and kisses."

—JONATHAN SWIFT

·Salads·

Warm Spring Salmon Salad	*Sixth Street Bistro & Loft*
Duck Breast Salad with Peaches and Hazelnuts	*Crush*
Organic Greens with Marionberry-Sage Vinaigrette	*Ashland Springs Hotel*
Red Grapefruit and Avocado Salad	*Harrison House Bed & Breakfast*
Pears with Goat Cheese, Pine Nuts, and Honey	*Mt. Ashland Inn*
Baby Spinach Salad with Poached Pears	*Gogi's Restaurant*
Olive Bread Salad	*Oliver's Twist*
Hail Caesar! Honeymoon Salad	*Woodmark Hotel*
Strawberry Spinach Salad	*The Honey Moon Cabin on Marrowstone Island*
Celery Root, Pear, and Hazelnut Salad	*The Herbfarm Restaurant*
Orecchiette Salad with Roasted Beets and Fennel	*Macrina Bakery & Cafe*
Green Goddess Wedge	*Place Pigalle*

Warm Spring Salmon Salad

SIXTH STREET BISTRO & LOFT, HOOD RIVER, OR

4 SERVINGS

How better to celebrate the Pacific Northwest than with organic greens, Pacific salmon, and fresh local asparagus? Just add a glass of chilled chenin blanc and a slice or two of great bread, and this can be quite a romantic dinner.

1. Blanch the asparagus in salted boiling water; plunge in an ice bath to preserve color and crispness. Drain and cut diagonally into 1-inch pieces.

2. To make a vinaigrette, in a food processor combine the vinegar, feta, and half of the chives; purée until smooth. Slowly add ½ cup of the olive oil in a thin stream to emulsify. Season to taste with salt and pepper.

3. Skin the salmon fillets and remove any dark brown flesh on the surface. In a large sauté pan, heat the remaining olive oil until the pan is hot, but not smoking. Sprinkle the fillets generously with salt and pepper. Place the fillets skinned side up in the pan and monitor the heat. The fillets should be seared on the bottom until they are a golden rusty brown. Turn the fillets over and remove the pan from the heat (they will continue to cook in the hot pan).

4. To assemble the salad, toss the greens with half of the asparagus and three-fourths of the vinaigrette. Arrange a small mound of the greens on each individual plate. Lean a salmon fillet gently against each mound of greens. Spoon the remaining asparagus around the plate. Garnish each plate with a drizzle of the remaining vinaigrette and a sprinkle of the remaining chives.

1 pound asparagus spears

¼ cup white wine vinegar or champagne vinegar

½ cup mild feta cheese

1 bunch chives, snipped, divided

½ cup plus 2 tablespoons olive oil, divided

Salt and freshly ground black pepper

Four 5-ounce wild salmon fillets, center cut

½ pound organic spring greens

Duck Breast Salad with Peaches and Hazelnuts

CRUSH, SEATTLE, WA   **6 SERVINGS**

Prepare this salad when peaches are at their freshest, July through September. The hazelnuts add a nice, flavorful crunch and complement the duck and peaches perfectly.

1. Cook the duck breasts, skin side down, in a cast iron or nonstick pan over medium heat until crispy, about 12 minutes. Turn the breasts over and cook for 2 more minutes. Transfer to a cutting board and reserve any fat in the pan. Let the duck rest for 4 minutes before cutting into thin slices.

2. To make a vinaigrette, in a small saucepan simmer both vinegars, the orange zest and juice, honey, and shallots until reduced to a third of the original volume; cool for a few minutes. Whisk in the olive oil and 3 tablespoons of the reserved duck fat. Add the thyme and set aside.

3. To assemble the salad, toss the arugula and endive with the vinaigrette. Arrange the dressed greens on individual plates. Top the greens with the duck, peaches, and hazelnuts. Season to taste with salt.

2 duck breasts (boneless, skin-on)

¼ cup sherry vinegar

¼ cup apple cider vinegar

Zest and juice of 2 oranges

1 teaspoon honey

2 shallots, finely minced

¼ cup olive oil

½ bunch thyme, finely chopped

1¼ pounds fresh arugula

2 heads Belgian endive

3 ripe peaches, peeled and sliced

½ cup toasted and skinned hazelnuts, chopped

Salt

Organic Greens with Marionberry-Sage Vinaigrette and Candied Hazelnuts

ASHLAND SPRINGS HOTEL, ASHLAND, OR

6 SERVINGS

You can refer to this as the perfect Oregon salad, with local, organic field greens, Oregon coast cranberries, Willamette Valley hazelnuts, and Oregon's marionberries in the vinaigrette.

1. Prepare the Candied Hazelnuts ahead of time. Toss the greens and cranberries with enough Marionberry-Sage Vinaigrette to coat the greens; sprinkle with Candied Hazelnuts.

Candied Hazelnuts (recipe follows)

10 ounces organic field greens

½ cup dried cranberries

Marionberry-Sage Vinaigrette (recipe follows)

Candied Hazelnuts

Preheat the oven to 350° F. Blanch the hazelnuts by boiling them in water for three minutes; drain. While still hot, toss the hazelnuts with the sugar, butter, and salt in a small bowl, until the butter is melted and the nuts are coated. Place the nuts on a raised-edge baking pan; bake for 12 minutes, stirring every 4 minutes. Remove from oven and let cool, stirring occasionally to prevent sticking.

1 cup whole hazelnuts

¼ cup packed brown sugar

1 teaspoon butter

1 teaspoon salt

Marionberry-Sage Vinaigrette

Combine the marionberries, sugar, vinegar, and water in a saucepan; cook over medium heat to reduce by half, about 10 minutes. Strain and let cool. Place in a blender with the sage and cayenne pepper. Blend over medium speed, slowly drizzling in the oil to emulsify. Season to taste with salt and pepper.

1 cup marionberries, fresh or frozen

¼ cup sugar

¼ cup rice wine vinegar

¼ cup water

½ teaspoon rubbed sage

⅛ teaspoon cayenne pepper

½ cup olive oil

Salt and freshly ground black pepper

Bring Home Flowers for You and Your Love

Long-lasting varieties:

Lilies: 7 to 14 days	Carnations: 7 to 14 days
Mums: 7 to 14 days	Delphiniums: 7 to 14 days
Zinnias: 6 to 14 days	Alstroemeria: 6 to 14 days
Sunflowers: 6 to 12 days	Orchids: 5 to 10 days
Daisies: 3 to 8 days	Roses: 3 to 7 days

Tips for extending the life of cut flowers:

Remove any leaves underwater.

Cut at least an additional ¼ inch from stems while underwater.

Always place roses in warm water. Use a good floral preservative.

Clean and refill the vase every day.

"The fragrance of the rose remains on the hand that gives it."

—UNKNOWN SOURCE

Red Grapefruit and Avocado Salad

HARRISON HOUSE BED & BREAKFAST, CORVALLIS, OR

6 SERVINGS

This is a relatively simple dish that looks great and can be served as a first course for breakfast or dinner. Serve it on individual plates or toss in a large bowl. The juicy grapefruit complements the silky smooth avocado, and the chili powder adds a zing to the citrus-lime marinade.

1. Segment the grapefruit, removing all skin, pith, and membranes (saving any juices); cut into bite-size pieces. Combine the grapefruit with the avocados in a medium bowl. In a small bowl, whisk together the lime juice, grapefruit juice, honey, and chili powder. Drizzle the juice mixture over the grapefruit and avocado, tossing gently.

2. Toast the coconut in a dry frying pan over medium-low heat until it just turns golden brown. Garnish the salad with the coconut.

4 medium red grapefruit

2 avocados, peeled, pitted, and chopped

3 tablespoons lime juice

3 tablespoons grapefruit juice (squeezed from above grapefruit)

1 teaspoon mild honey

¼ teaspoon chili powder

½ cup sweetened shredded coconut

Pears with Goat Cheese, Pine Nuts, and Honey

MT. ASHLAND INN, ASHLAND, OR   **2 SERVINGS**

This simple salad is light and refreshing. It's a perfect salad to serve for brunch or as a first course for dinner.

1. Place a handful of greens on each of two small plates. Fan out pear slices on the greens. Using a fork, flake the goat cheese over the pears; sprinkle with the pine nuts. Drizzle with the honey; garnish with grated orange peel. Serve immediately.

Baby greens

1 just-ripe pear, sliced

1 tablespoon goat cheese

2 tablespoons pine nuts, toasted

1 tablespoon warm honey

Grated orange peel

Romantic Picnic-Basket Fare

Brie cheese and French bread
Marinated olives
Green apples and smoked cheddar cheese
Veggies and dip
Red and green grapes
Dried apricots
Hummus and pita bread
Pistachio nuts
Smoked oysters and crackers
Pepperidge Farms Milano cookies

"You know it's love when the everyday things surrounding you—the leaves, the shade of light in the sky, a bowl of strawberries—suddenly shimmer with a kind of unreality."

—JOAN GATTUSO

Baby Spinach Salad with Poached Pears, Candied Pecans, and Oregon Blue Cheese

GOGI'S RESTAURANT, JACKSONVILLE, OR

8 SERVINGS

Th" is a spectacular salad to make when you want to impress guests. Don't be intimidated, as much of it can be done ahead of time. Any left-over pecans can be used on another salad or just for snacking.

1. To prepare the poached pears, preheat the oven to 400°F. Combine the wine and water in a 9- by 13-inch baking dish. Add the sugar and salt and stir until dissolved. Place the pears in the baking dish, cut side down. Add the cinnamon stick and anise pods; cover tightly with foil. Bake until the pears are tender when pierced with a knife, 20 to 30 minutes. Remove from oven and let cool completely in the poaching liquid, about 1½ hours.

2. Meanwhile, prepare the Candied Pecans and the Red Wine–Shallot Vinaigrette.

3. To assemble the salads, toss the spinach with enough vinaigrette to coat the leaves; divide among eight salad plates. Fan the poached pear halves by partially cutting into six to seven slices lengthwise; set one pear half on each salad. Sprinkle the salads with the Candied Pecans and blue cheese.

2 cups white wine

1 cup hot water

½ cup sugar

Pinch of salt

4 semifirm Anjou pears, peeled, cut in half, and cored

1 cinnamon stick

2 star anise pods or ¼ teaspoon five-spice powder

1 cup Candied Pecans (recipe follows)

Red Wine–Shallot Vinaigrette (recipe follows)

1 pound fresh baby spinach leaves

1 cup Rogue Creamery "Oregon Blue" cheese, crumbled

Candied Pecans

Preheat the oven to 250° F. Combine the sugar, nutmeg, cinnamon, pepper, and salt in a small bowl; mix thoroughly. In a small bowl, beat the egg white until frothy. Toss the pecans gently in egg white to coat. Gently toss the pecans with the sugar-spice mixture, stirring to coat evenly. Spread the nuts in a single layer on a foil-lined raised-edge baking pan. Bake for 50 minutes, stirring every 15 minutes, until the nuts are toasted and dry to the touch. Cool completely, about 1 hour.

½ cup sugar

Pinch of freshly ground nutmeg

½ teaspoon ground cinnamon

¼ teaspoon white pepper

¼ teaspoon ground chipotle powder

⅛ teaspoon salt

1 egg white

2 cups pecan halves

Red Wine–Shallot Vinaigrette

In a small bowl, whisk together the shallot, vinegar, mustard, and sugar. Slowly add the oil while whisking until it emulsifies. Season to taste with salt and pepper.

½ tablespoon minced shallot

¼ cup red wine vinegar

½ tablespoon Dijon mustard

1 tablespoon sugar

¾ cup olive oil

Salt and freshly ground black pepper

Olive Bread Salad

OLIVER'S TWIST, SEATTLE, WA **4 SERVINGS**

Here is a wonderful way to use leftover bread from last night's supper. This recipe brings together fresh Italian ingredients in a bowl of perfect harmony that any salad gourmand will appreciate.

1. Cut five 1-inch-thick slices of olive bread. Heat the olive oil in a large skillet over medium heat until shimmering. Add the bread slices and fry on each side until golden brown, about 2 minutes per side. Drain on paper towels. After 1 minute, while the bread is still warm, cut the slices into 1-inch croutons. Place the warm croutons in a large mixing bowl; add the pine nuts, mozzarella, tomatoes, arugula, and half of the Parmigiano. Toss with the pesto and Whole Grain Mustard Vinaigrette. Sprinkle the salad with the remaining cheese.

½ loaf olive bread

½ cup olive oil

½ cup pine nuts

6 ounces fresh bocconcini mozzarella balls cut in half

½ cup cherry or grape tomatoes, cut in half

6 ounces baby arugula

¼ cup grated Parmigiano-Reggiano cheese, divided

¼ cup basil pesto

¼ cup Whole Grain Mustard Vinaigrette (recipe follows)

Whole Grain Mustard Vinaigrette

In a small bowl, whisk together the mustard, shallot, and vinegar. Slowly drizzle in the olive oil, whisking to combine. Season to taste with salt and pepper.

2 tablespoons whole grain mustard

½ tablespoon minced shallot

¼ cup red wine vinegar

¼ cup olive oil

Salt and freshly ground black pepper

Hail Caesar! Honeymoon Salad

WOODMARK HOTEL, KIRKLAND, WA — **2 SERVINGS**

At the Woodmark Hotel, this salad is served in three variations: honeymoon style ("lettuce alone"), with smoked salmon, and with grilled chicken. The hard-boiled eggs are used to reduce the risk of salmonella (and, surprisingly, the dressing does get smooth). The dressing will keep, refrigerated, for about a week.

1. Toss the lettuce with Caesar dressing; add the croutons. Season to taste with pepper. Sprinkle with Parmesan cheese.

1 large or 2 small bunches of romaine lettuce, torn into bite-size pieces

Caesar Dressing (recipe follows)

Croutons (optional)

Freshly ground black pepper

2 tablespoons freshly grated Parmesan cheese

Caesar Dressing

Place the oil, lemon juice, Parmesan, egg, anchovy, mustard, Tabasco, Worcestershire, garlic, and salt in a blender and process until smooth.

⅓ cup olive oil

3 tablespoons fresh lemon juice

½ cup shredded Parmesan cheese

1 hard-boiled egg, peeled

1 anchovy fillet

1 teaspoon Dijon mustard

½ teaspoon green or regular Tabasco

¼ teaspoon Worcestershire sauce

1 garlic clove, minced

½ teaspoon salt

Strawberry Spinach Salad

2 SERVINGS

This salad is equally delicious using fresh blueberries in place of the strawberries. For a "dynamite" Fourth of July salad, use both blueberries and strawberries and create a Red, White, and Blue–Berry Salad. Put the salad in a large glass bowl and toss with the dressing just before serving.

1. To assemble the salad, divide the spinach leaves evenly between two plates. Top with the strawberries, feta, nuts, and onion. Drizzle with Poppy Seed Dressing just before serving.

4 cups fresh baby spinach leaves

¾ cup sliced fresh strawberries

¼ cup feta cheese, crumbled

¼ cup sliced almonds or walnuts, toasted

4 to 6 thinly sliced red onion rings

Poppy Seed Dressing (recipe follows)

Poppy Seed Dressing

Whisk together the oil, sugar, vinegars, seeds, onion, and paprika until well blended.

2 tablespoons olive oil

2 tablespoons sugar

1 tablespoon cider vinegar

1 tablespoon red wine vinegar

½ tablespoon sesame seeds

1 teaspoon poppy seeds

½ teaspoon dried minced onion

⅛ teaspoon paprika

Celery Root, Pear, and Hazelnut Salad

THE HERBFARM RESTAURANT, WOODINVILLE, WA

6 SERVINGS

Celery root, also called celeriac, is a rather ugly, knobby brown vegetable that tastes like a cross between a strong celery and parsley. It can be eaten raw or cooked. Celery root has recently gained in popularity, and this is a wonderful way to be introduced to it.

1. Cut the celery root into julienne slices, using a mandoline or the shredding blade on a food processor, or coarsely grate it using a box grater; set aside. Whisk the vinegar, mustard, thyme, and salt in a medium bowl. Slowly whisk in the oils. Add the celery root; toss well. Refrigerate for at least one hour.

2. Meanwhile, use a mandoline or a sharp knife to thinly slice the celery. Julienne, shred, or grate the pear in the same manner as the celery root. Toss the celery and pear with the celery root. Serve the salad in a serving bowl or divide it onto individual plates. Sprinkle with the hazelnuts and cheese.

1 large (12 to 16 ounces) celery root, peeled

¼ cup sherry vinegar

3 tablespoons whole grain Dijon-style mustard

2 teaspoons coarsely chopped fresh thyme leaves

1 teaspoon salt

¼ cup olive oil

¼ cup hazelnut oil

3 stalks celery

1 large unpeeled Bosc pear, ripe but firm

½ cup hazelnuts, toasted and chopped

Grated pecorino Romano cheese

Orecchiette Salad with Roasted Beets and Fennel

MACRINA BAKERY & CAFE, SEATTLE, WA **6 SERVINGS**

Orecchiette pasta is a distinctive Puglian type of pasta shaped roughly like small ears, hence the name (*orecchiette*: Italian for little ears). They're about ¾ of an inch across and slightly domed in the middle. The cup shape serves to hold the vinaigrette, making every bite extra flavorful. This is a wonderful year-round pasta salad that makes an appearance in the *Macrina Bakery & Cafe Cookbook* and is very popular at Macrina's take-out café.

1. Preheat the oven to 350°F. Place the beets in the center of a large piece of foil; drizzle them with 2 tablespoons of the olive oil. Gather up the edges of the foil, sealing the beets inside a pouch. Bake on the center rack of the oven for 1 hour, or until fork-tender. When cool, peel the beets and dice into ½-inch cubes. Set aside.

2. Cook the pasta according to package directions; drain. Mix the pasta with the remaining olive oil. In a large bowl, combine the almonds, radicchio, fennel bulb and fronds, green onions, and parsley. Add the pasta and Lemon Vinaigrette; stir to combine. Season to taste with salt and pepper. Serve the salad at room temperature, or refrigerate for up to 2 days and serve chilled. (Note: The salad can be made up to 2 days ahead and refrigerated.)

2 to 3 medium golden beets, scrubbed

4 tablespoons olive oil, divided

2 cups dry orecchiette pasta

¾ cup whole almonds, toasted and coarsely chopped

1 cup thinly sliced radicchio

½ cup thinly sliced fennel bulb

¼ cup chopped fennel fronds

½ cup diced green onions

¼ cup fresh Italian parsley

Lemon Vinaigrette (recipe follows)

Salt and freshly ground black pepper

Lemon Vinaigrette

In a small bowl, whisk together the lemon zest and juice, vinegar, mustard, honey, garlic, salt, and pepper. Add the olive oil in a slow stream, whisking until the dressing has emulsified. (Note: Vinaigrette can be made ahead and refrigerated for up to 4 days.)

1 teaspoon grated lemon zest

2 tablespoons freshly squeezed lemon juice

1 teaspoon red wine vinegar

1 teaspoon Dijon mustard

½ teaspoon honey

1 clove garlic, finely chopped

½ teaspoon salt

⅛ teaspoon pepper

¼ cup olive oil

Green Goddess Wedge

PLACE PIGALLE, SEATTLE, WA   **4 TO 6 SERVINGS**

The dressing is also a great dip to serve with crudités — try it with strips of jicama, endive leaves, and baby carrots.

1. In a food processor, process the parsley, tarragon, mustard, lemon juice, and anchovies until well blended. Fold in the crème fraîche. Season to taste with salt and pepper. Add water in increments, stirring well, until the dressing reaches the desired consistency.

2. Dress a wedge of iceberg or a salad of Bibb or romaine with the dressing. Garnish with fresh tomatoes and the remaining chopped parsley.

1 bunch parsley, coarsely chopped (reserve a little for garnish)

2 bunches fresh tarragon leaves, tough stems removed

2 tablespoons Dijon mustard

2 tablespoons freshly squeezed lemon juice

1 can (2 ounces) anchovy fillets with oil

½ cup crème fraîche

Salt and freshly ground pepper

Lettuce (iceberg, Bibb, romaine)

Tomatoes (optional)

Main Courses

Curried Lentil Soup with Coriander Lime Cream	*Stephanie Inn*
Creamy Beet Risotto	*Tulio Ristorante*
Bachelor's Pasta	*Cor Cellars*
Cold Farm Day Chicken Stew	*Betty MacDonald Farm*
Warm Chicken Baguette Sandwiches	*Vin du Lac Winery*
Chicken Roulade	*Bonneville Hot Springs Resort & Spa*
Cougar Gold Chicken	*Bonair Winery*
Chicken Cacciatore	*Il Fiasco*
Pollo Blu	*Assaggio Ristorante*
Pappardelle Pasta	*Cork*
Lemon Risotto with Garlic Prawns and Snap Peas	*Torii Mor Winery*
Canlis Prawns	*Canlis Restaurant*
Halibut Crab Cakes	*Cuvée Restaurant*
Dungeness Crab Mac and Cheese with Hazelnut Crust	*Sybaris*
Crab Fettuccine with Wild Mushrooms	*Baked Alaska*
Garlic Shrimp Pasta	*Lonesome Cove Resort*
Pan-Fried Oysters with Garlic Aioli	*The Depot Restaurant*
Seared Scallops with Corn, Pancetta, and Green Onions	*King Estate Winery*
Northwest Bouillabaisse	*The Blue Heron Inn*
Pasta Puttanesca with Ahi Tuna	*Serafina Osteria & Enoteca*
Grilled Italian Tuna Steaks	*Cozy Rose Inn Bed and Breakfast*
Alice Bay Barbecued Salmon	*Alice Bay Bed & Breakfast*
Grilled Salmon with Raspberry and Tarragon Butter Sauce	*Markus' Wharfside Restaurant*
Halibut with Hazelnut Sauce	*Silverwater Café*
Black Cod, Sweet Corn, and Fava Beans	*Celilo Restaurant*
Pistachio-Crusted Sablefish with Roasted Red Pepper Sauce	*Quattro at Whistler*
Grilled Turkey Tenderloin with Sage Pesto	*Abbey Road Farm*
Pork Tenderloin with Caramelized Balsamic Onions	*Blue Fjord Cabins*
Mama's Meatballs	*The Pink Door*
Chateaubriand for Two	*El Gaucho*
Pan-Seared Duck Breast with Roasted Tomato Relish	*Brentwood Bay Lodge & Spa*
Grilled Lamb Chops with Hazelnut Romesco Sauce	*Marché*
Venison Tenderloin with Parsnip Purée	*Freestone Inn*

Curried Lentil Soup with Coriander Lime Cream

STEPHANIE INN, CANNON BEACH, OR   **8 SERVINGS**

Marvel at the flavors that magically come together in an explosion of deliciousness. Homemade soups like this are perhaps the perfect winter dish to warm you from the inside out.

1. Heat the olive oil in a Dutch oven over medium heat. Add the onion and garlic; cook, stirring occasionally, until the onions are translucent, about 5 minutes. Add the tomatoes, lentils, curry powder, and vegetable stock; bring to a boil. Turn heat to low and cook, covered, until the lentils are tender, about 40 minutes.

2. Add the basil and lemon juice to the soup just before serving. (Note: You may purée the soup at this point if you'd like.) Season to taste with salt and pepper. Serve the soup in bowls with a dollop of the Coriander Lime Cream.

2 tablespoons olive oil

2 cups chopped onion

1½ teaspoons minced garlic

4 plum tomatoes, chopped

1 cup dried lentils, rinsed

1 tablespoon yellow curry powder

8 cups vegetable or chicken stock

2 to 3 tablespoons chopped fresh basil

1 tablespoon freshly squeezed lemon juice

Salt and freshly ground black pepper

Coriander Lime Cream (recipe follows)

Coriander Lime Cream

Mix the creams, coriander, and lime zest and juice together in a small bowl until well combined.

¼ cup sour cream

2 tablespoons heavy cream

¾ teaspoon ground coriander

Zest and juice of 1 small lime

Creamy Beet Risotto

TULIO RISTORANTE, SEATTLE, WA

4 SERVINGS

Revel in the bright, beautiful fuchsia color of this dish (think Valentine's Day), and you'll come to appreciate that it's not just tastiness, but a high level of comfort that this risotto provides.

1. Preheat the oven to 450°F. Tightly wrap the beets in a double layer of foil; roast on a baking sheet for 1½ hours, or until the beets are tender when pierced with a knife. Cool for 10 minutes. Wearing protective gloves, wash the beets under cool running water and slip off the skins. Dice the beets and set aside.

2. In a heavy-bottomed Dutch oven, melt the butter over medium-high heat. Add the onion and cook until soft, stirring frequently, about 5 minutes. Add the rice and stir for 1 minute to toast. Add 1 cup of the broth and stir until all the liquid is absorbed. Continue adding the broth, 1 cup at a time, stirring after each addition, until the broth is absorbed (approximately 10 to 15 minutes between each addition of broth).

3. The risotto is done when the grains are tender and plump but still have a little bite. (This process should take about 4 cups of broth.) If the rice is still crunchy, continue to add broth in small amounts until the risotto has a creamy consistency. Stir in the beets. Season to taste with salt and pepper. Serve in individual bowls, sprinkled with the Gorgonzola and pine nuts.

---

8 small red or gold beets, scrubbed

¼ cup (½ stick) butter

1 medium yellow onion, finely diced

1½ cups arborio rice

4 to 5 cups vegetable broth

Salt and freshly ground black pepper

¼ cup crumbled Gorgonzola cheese

¼ cup pine nuts, toasted

Bachelor's Pasta

COR CELLARS, LYLE, WA   **2 SERVINGS**

This recipe from Tuscany is called Bachelor's Pasta because it is easy to cook and can be made after a long night out. If you like your sauce with a little kick, use the fresh jalapeño pepper—otherwise, add red pepper flakes to taste.

1. Heat the oil in a medium skillet over medium heat. Add the garlic; cook until it begins to turn golden, stirring frequently. Stir in the tomatoes. Add the anchovy; smash it with the back of a spoon to help distribute it in the sauce. Stir in the jalapeño and rosemary. Add the tomato paste and sugar; stir until incorporated. Bring to a simmer; let cook at low heat for 20 to 30 minutes, stirring occasionally. Add water as necessary to prevent the sauce from getting too thick.

2. Meanwhile, cook the pasta according to package directions until al dente; drain. Place the pasta in a serving bowl; toss with the sauce and olive oil to taste. Sprinkle with Parmesan and serve.

1 tablespoon olive oil plus additional for serving

8 cloves garlic, coarsely chopped

1 pound plum tomatoes, diced, or one 14.5-ounce can diced tomatoes, undrained

1 anchovy (from a can or jar, with olive oil)

1 small red jalapeño pepper, seeded, ribs removed, and finely chopped, or red pepper flakes to taste

2 teaspoons fresh chopped rosemary

1 tablespoons tomato paste (sun-dried or regular)

1 to 2 teaspoons sugar

¼ to ½ cup water or dry red wine

2½ cups uncooked penne or other pasta

Freshly grated Parmesan cheese (optional)

Cold Farm Day Chicken Stew

BETTY MACDONALD FARM, VASHON ISLAND, WA · **4 SERVINGS**

Massively good, this warm-you-up stew uses spices and vegetables to their best advantage. Tender, succulent chicken pairs perfectly with the moist comfort of sweet potatoes or squash. Stir in some fresh steamed broccoli just before serving for extra color and goodness.

1. Put the chicken in a medium bowl and cover evenly with the lemon juice, cumin, allspice, and cayenne pepper; set aside.

2. Heat the oil over medium heat in large heavy saucepan or Dutch oven. Add the garlic, onions, and sweet potatoes; cook for 5 minutes, stirring frequently. Add the spiced chicken and cook for 4 to 5 minutes, stirring frequently, until the exterior is no longer pink. Add the stock and garbanzo beans; bring to a boil. Lower heat; cover and simmer until the chicken is cooked all the way through and the vegetables are tender, about 15 minutes.

3. Season to taste with salt and pepper. Serve in bowls over couscous, if desired. Garnish with parsley and lemon slices.

1½ pounds boned chicken thighs, cut into 1½-inch chunks

3 tablespoons freshly squeezed lemon juice

1 teaspoon ground cumin

½ teaspoon ground allspice

¼ to ½ teaspoon cayenne pepper

2 tablespoons olive oil

2 cloves garlic, minced

1 medium red onion, chopped

4 green onions, chopped

2 to 3 large sweet potatoes or 1 medium butternut squash, peeled and cut into 1-inch cubes

2 cups chicken stock

One 15.5-ounce can garbanzo beans, drained

Salt and freshly ground black pepper

4 cups cooked couscous (optional)

Fresh chopped parsley or cilantro

Lemon slices

Warm Chicken Baguette Sandwiches

VIN DU LAC WINERY, CHELAN, WA

4 SANDWICHES

These are tasty mouthfuls of barbecued bliss meant to be shared by lovers eating from the same plate and sipping glasses of Vin du Lac chardonnay together. The full-bodied, crisp texture and buttery flavors of the wine are excellent complements to the smoky earthiness and spice of the sandwich. Enjoy them both outside on a warm Pacific Northwest summer evening.

Four 6-inch baguettes, cut in half lengthwise

Sesame Garlic Mayonnaise (recipe follows)

1 cup shredded Grilled Smoked Chicken (recipe follows)

1 medium sweet onion, thinly sliced and sautéed in butter

4 slices Havarti cheese

1 fresh jalapeño pepper, seeded, ribs removed, sliced into rings (optional)

Fresh cilantro sprigs

1. Lightly toast or warm the baguettes. Spread Sesame Garlic Mayonnaise on the cut sides of both halves of the baguettes. Layer each sandwich with ¼ cup shredded chicken, 2 heaping tablespoons of sautéed onions, 1 slice of cheese, 3 or 4 jalapeño slices, and a couple of sprigs of cilantro. Cut the sandwiches in half diagonally. Serve warm.

Sesame Garlic Mayonnaise

Combine the mayonnaise, garlic, and oil in a small bowl; stir well.

¼ cup mayonnaise

¼ teaspoon minced garlic

¼ teaspoon sesame oil

Grilled Smoked Chicken

Start a charcoal fire. Coat the chicken breasts lightly with the oil; season liberally with salt, pepper, and Italian seasoning. Add several thick pieces of green apple wood to the fire immediately before grilling. Place the breasts on the grill, bone side down. Cook for 30 to 40 minutes, making sure good smoke is generated for at least 20 minutes. Turn the breasts so the meat side is down. Cook for 30 minutes, or until the chicken is no longer pink inside when sliced. Remove the chicken meat from the bone; shred with a fork and knife or your hands.

2 bone-in chicken breasts

1 tablespoon vegetable oil

Salt and freshly ground black pepper

½ teaspoon Italian seasoning

Apple wood for smoking

Romance Without Cooking

Serve one or more of this smorgasbord of sensual delights:

Bowl of smoked almonds
Plate of olives, cheese, salami, crackers
Fresh oysters with grated horseradish and lemon
Chilled blanched asparagus with wasabi mayonnaise
Jumbo shrimp and a bowl of cocktail sauce
Fresh warm baguette with plate of truffle oil and balsamic vinegar
Plate of fresh figs, blue cheese, and walnuts drizzled with honey
Fresh strawberries dipped in crème fraîche and brown sugar
Chunks of organic dark chocolate and crystallized ginger

"Nothing would be so sweet as whipped cream on your lips;
makes for a very nice treat, and a very tasty kiss!"

—UNKNOWN SOURCE

Chicken Roulade

BONNEVILLE HOT SPRINGS RESORT & SPA, NORTH BONNEVILLE, WA

2 SERVINGS

With each slice displaying a colorful garland of filling, this roulade is impressive enough to serve on the good china. The filling can be adapted to the season; in the winter, for example, think sun-dried tomatoes, feta cheese, and pine nuts.

1. Preheat the oven to 350° F. Heat the butter and oil in a medium skillet over medium heat. Add the shallots and mushrooms; cook until the mushrooms turn golden brown, about 10 minutes. Stir in the spinach; cook until slightly wilted. Deglaze with the wine. Let cool.

2. Cut two 6-inch squares of parchment paper and two 12-inch squares of aluminum foil; center a parchment square on each foil square. Brush the parchment with the melted butter; sprinkle with the rosemary, sage, and parsley. Place the chicken breasts between two pieces of plastic wrap; using a meat mallet, carefully pound the chicken to about ¼ inch thick; sprinkle with salt and pepper. Place each chicken breast in the center of a parchment square.

3. Mix the mushroom mixture with the egg, bread crumbs, and cheese. Divide the mixture evenly and pat into the centers of the breasts. Roll up the chicken, jelly roll–style, in the parchment and then the foil. Bake for 22 to 25 minutes, or until heated through.

4. To serve, remove the parchment and foil and place each chicken breast on an individual plate. Garnish with fresh herbs.

½ tablespoon butter

½ tablespoon olive oil

1 tablespoon minced shallots

1¼ cups sliced cremini mushrooms

4 cups baby spinach leaves

2 tablespoons dry white wine

1 tablespoon butter, melted

1 teaspoon chopped fresh rosemary

1 teaspoon chopped fresh sage

1 teaspoon chopped fresh parsley

2 skinless, boneless chicken breasts

Salt and freshly ground black pepper

1 egg, slightly beaten

⅓ cup panko (Japanese-style) bread crumbs

⅓ cup grated white cheddar cheese

Additional fresh herbs (optional)

Cougar Gold Chicken

BONAIR WINERY, ZILLAH, WA **2 SERVINGS**

Perhaps the perfect nuptial feast—a richly balanced dish of chicken, cheese, and wine. You don't have to be a Cougar fan to declare this dish a winner! Serve it with rice and asparagus for an amazingly simple, scrumptious dinner.

1. Preheat the oven to 350° F. Season the chicken with salt and pepper; coat in flour. Melt the butter in a medium skillet over medium heat. Cook the chicken until golden brown on both sides, 4 to 5 minutes. Place the chicken in a baking dish and sprinkle with nutmeg and cayenne pepper. Bake for 20 to 25 minutes, or until the chicken is no longer pink in the center.

2. While the chicken is baking, deglaze the pan with the wine over medium heat, loosening any bits of chicken left in the pan. Reduce heat. In a small bowl, mix the crème fraîche and egg yolk; whisk into the wine. Add the cheese and blend thoroughly, adding more wine as needed to make a creamy sauce.

3. When the chicken comes out of the oven, set the oven to broil. Spoon the cheese sauce over the breasts; broil until the cheese starts to turn golden (watch closely), about 1 minute.

2 skinless, boneless chicken breasts

Salt and freshly ground black pepper

½ cup all-purpose flour

1 tablespoon butter

Pinch of freshly ground nutmeg

Pinch of cayenne pepper

¼ cup Bonair Rattlesnake Hills Riesling, plus additional if needed

¼ cup crème fraîche

1 egg yolk

¾ cup shredded Cougar Gold or other white sharp cheddar cheese

Chicken Cacciatore

IL FIASCO, TACOMA, WA   **4 SERVINGS**

This dish is a good one to cook as friends gather in the kitchen for a glass of wine before dinner (you'll need to open the wine for the sauce, so . . .). The sauce is quite thick and takes some time to reduce, so plan accordingly. The aromas from the reduction are heavenly, and the flavor is divine. Serve with polenta or mashed potatoes.

Cacciatore Sauce (see Note; recipe follows)

4 skinless, boneless chicken breasts

Salt and pepper

1. Prepare the Cacciatore Sauce.

2. To bake the chicken, preheat the oven to 350°F. Grease or spray a baking dish with cooking spray. Season the chicken with salt and pepper; put in the baking dish. Bake for 25 minutes, or until the chicken is no longer pink in the center.

3. To serve, spoon the Cacciatore Sauce over the chicken breasts.

Note: The cacciatore sauce takes approximately 2 hours to cook. Start baking the chicken toward the end of the cacciatore sauce reduction to ensure that the sauce and chicken are done around the same time. If necessary, the sauce can be kept warm over low heat—just add a splash of red wine or water to keep it from thickening too much.

Cacciatore Sauce

In a large sauté pan, cook the peppers and onion on low heat for 10 to 15 minutes, stirring frequently, to allow them to "sweat" without additional liquid. (Adjust heat if peppers start burning.) Add the garlic; deglaze with the wine. Let the wine reduce until almost all of the liquid is gone, 30 to 35 minutes. Add the stock and reduce until almost all of the liquid is gone, 30 to 35 minutes. Add the tomatoes with juice, brown sugar, vinegar, oregano, and bay leaf. Simmer for 1 hour on low heat, stirring occasionally so the sauce does not stick to the pan. Season to taste with salt and pepper. Remove the bay leaf. Stir in the butter to finish the sauce.

1 red bell pepper, julienned

1 green bell pepper, julienned

1 yellow bell pepper, julienned

1 small red onion, julienned

6 cloves garlic, finely chopped

2 cups dry red wine

2 cups chicken stock

One 14.5-ounce can diced tomatoes with juice

1 tablespoon brown sugar

1 teaspoon balsamic vinegar

1 tablespoon chopped fresh oregano leaves

1 bay leaf

Salt and freshly ground black pepper

2 tablespoons butter

Pollo Blu

2 SERVINGS

This is a profoundly simple dish with knock-your-socks-off flavor. The best part: it doesn't take much time to prepare, which leaves more time for the two of you to spend together. Serve it with a side of orzo, steamed broccoli, and a hearty red wine. *Salut!*

1. Preheat the oven to 375° F. Heat the olive oil in a medium ovenproof sauté pan over medium heat. Pan-sear the chicken, about 4 minutes per side. Add the wine; reduce heat. Cover and simmer for 8 to 10 minutes until the liquid is almost gone. Stir in the Gorgonzola and cream. Bake for 15 minutes, or until chicken is no longer pink in the center. Sprinkle with parsley and season to taste with pepper.

1 tablespoon olive oil

2 boneless chicken breasts

¼ cup dry white wine

3 ounces Gorgonzola cheese, diced

1 cup heavy cream

1 tablespoon finely chopped fresh Italian parsley

Freshly ground black pepper

How to Celebrate All Year Long

Here's a romantic suggestion that will last you throughout the year. Buy a case of prosecco (Italian bubbly) and label each bottle with dates: (Don't forget to put these on your calendar!)

Valentine's Day	Your birthdays
Anniversary of the day you met	The next full moon
First day of spring	Summer solstice
Sweetest Day (third Saturday in October)	Personal or work accomplishment
First snowfall	Winter solstice (longest night!)
Christmas morning	New Year's Eve

"Having you to love is reason enough to celebrate."

—UNKNOWN SOURCE

Pappardelle Pasta

CORK, BEND, OR **4 SERVINGS**

Pappardelle (pa-par-DAY-lay) are flat ribbons of pasta, normally served with hearty sauces. Fresh pasta is best, but in a pinch you can substitute dried wide egg noodles. The sauce bursts with an amazing fusion of flavors—a bit like slurping a spicy orange Creamsicle. You can interchange vegetables too, substituting roasted red peppers for the tomatoes, adding steamed broccoli, and so on.

1. Cook the pasta according to package directions until al dente. Drain and keep warm.

2. Heat the oil over high heat in a large sauté pan. Add the chicken, salt, and pepper, and cook, stirring occasionally, until golden brown, 3 to 4 minutes. Add the prawns and jalapeños; cook until the prawns turn pink, 1 to 2 minutes. Remove the chicken and prawns; keep warm. Add the wine; cook until reduced by half. Whisk in the stock, orange juice concentrate, cream, Tabasco, and salt and pepper; bring to a boil. Reduce heat and simmer for 5 to 7 minutes, until the sauce slightly thickens. Add the chicken, prawns, and tomatoes; stir until heated through. Stir in the cooked pasta.

3. Serve in individual pasta bowls, sprinkled with cilantro and garnished with lime wedges.

One 9-ounce package fresh pappardelle, tagliatelle, or fettuccine

2 tablespoons vegetable oil

¾ pound skinless, boneless chicken breasts, cut into 1-inch cubes

¼ teaspoon salt

⅛ teaspoon freshly ground black pepper

½ pound prawns (31 to 40 per pound), peeled and deveined

1 large or 2 small jalapeño peppers, seeded, ribs removed, and chopped

¼ cup white wine

⅔ cup fish stock or clam juice

½ cup orange juice concentrate

⅔ cup heavy cream

Few dashes of Tabasco or other hot sauce

Salt and freshly ground black pepper

3 plum tomatoes, diced

2 tablespoons chopped fresh cilantro

Fresh lime wedges (optional)

Lemon Risotto with Garlic Prawns and Snap Peas

TORII MOR WINERY, DUNDEE, OR

2 SERVINGS

Risotto is a little labor intensive, but you can devote all of your attention to getting it just right, then cover it, and it will stay warm while the prawns and sugar snap peas cook up in just a few minutes. Pair this with a lovely bottle of Torii Mor pinot blanc or chardonnay.

1. In a small saucepan, heat the stock and keep warm over low heat. In a medium skillet, heat the oil over medium heat. Add the shallots; cook until transparent, about 3 minutes. Add the rice; sauté for 2 minutes, stirring frequently. Add the wine and let reduce until almost all of the liquid is gone, stirring frequently. Add one cup of hot stock to the rice and cook, stirring frequently, until the rice has absorbed most of the liquid. Continue to add stock, ½ cup at a time, stirring frequently, and allowing each addition to be absorbed before the next is added.

2. When the rice is cooked through but still has a "bite," turn off heat and add the Parmesan, lemon zest and juice, and parsley. Top the risotto with the Garlic Prawns and Snap Peas before serving.

3½ cups chicken stock

2 tablespoons olive oil

2 tablespoons finely chopped shallots

1 cup arborio rice

½ cup dry white wine

½ cup grated Parmesan cheese

Zest and juice of 1 lemon

2 tablespoons chopped parsley

Garlic Prawns and Snap Peas (recipe follows)

Garlic Prawns and Snap Peas

In a large sauté pan, heat the butter and oil over medium-high heat. Add the garlic and pepper flakes; cook until fragrant, about 15 seconds. Add the prawns; cook, stirring frequently, about 4 minutes, or until pink on both sides. Add the peas and cook until they are heated through, 3 to 4 minutes. Season to taste with salt. Sprinkle with a squeeze of fresh lemon juice.

½ tablespoon butter

1 tablespoon olive oil

1 to 2 garlic cloves, chopped

¼ teaspoon red pepper flakes (optional)

¾ to 1 pound prawns (31 to 40 per pound), peeled and deveined

½ pound sugar snap peas

Salt

½ small lemon

Ingredients for Intimate Dining

Turn down the overhead lights.
Burn nonscented candles.
Remember fresh flowers.
Dance in the kitchen.
Sit down together.
Eat by candlelight.
Play soft music.

"One cannot think well, love well, sleep well, if one has not dined well."
—VIRGINIA WOOLF

Canlis Prawns

CANLIS RESTAURANT, SEATTLE, WA

2 SERVINGS

From one of Seattle's classic romantic restaurants come these unforgettable, quintessential sautéed prawns. These have been on the menu for nearly fifty years, and it's no surprise—they boast a big sassy flavor and practically melt in your mouth.

1. Heat the oil in a stainless steel pan over high heat. Just before the oil reaches the smoking point, add the prawns and season with salt and pepper; sear the prawns on both sides. As soon as the prawns turn pink, pour off the excess oil. Return the pan to the stove; reduce the heat to medium. Add the garlic and stir just until it begins to turn golden brown. Remove the pan from the heat and deglaze with the vermouth and lime juice. Add the pepper flakes.

2. Return the pan to the heat and stir, reducing the liquid by half. Add the Shrimp Butter; taste and adjust seasonings. Remove the prawns and arrange on a platter surrounding the greens. Drizzle any sauce left in the pan over the prawns.

2 tablespoons olive oil

12 black tiger prawns (16 to 20 per pound), shells removed and reserved for Shrimp Butter

Salt and freshly ground black pepper

½ teaspoon minced garlic

¼ cup extra-dry vermouth

1½ teaspoons freshly squeezed lime juice

½ teaspoon red pepper flakes

¼ cup Shrimp Butter (recipe follows)

Baby greens

Shrimp Butter

Preheat the oven to 500°F. Place the prawn shells in a baking pan and roast for 3 minutes, or until the shells turn pink. Remove the tails and legs. Melt the butter until boiling hot. Place the shells in a blender with an equal amount of the boiling hot butter. Blend for several minutes, until the shells have completely broken down. Strain the butter and shell mixture through a fine mesh strainer; discard the shells. Chill the butter in an ice bath, whisking until it thickens. Keep at room temperature.

12 reserved black tiger prawn shells

½ cup (1 stick) butter

Halibut Crab Cakes

4 SERVINGS

Crab cakes make a wonderful light supper or brunch entrée. These have the elegant addition of halibut, giving them a slightly more robust flavor. Serve with Caesar salad, crusty bread, and a chilled bottle of white wine. Lump crabmeat in 1-pound cans is often sold in the refrigerated section of grocery stores.

1. In a food processor, finely chop the halibut; continue chopping for about 2 minutes. Add the mayonnaise, egg, garlic, lemon peel and juice, peppers, and nutmeg; process until blended. Add the cream; blend until the mixture becomes a thick paste. Transfer the mixture to a medium bowl; gently fold in the crabmeat, Old Bay Spice, and salt.

2. Form the crab mixture into 12 round patties. Heat the butter in a medium skillet over medium heat. Fry the patties until golden brown on the bottom, 3 to 4 minutes. Carefully turn the patties. Flatten slightly with a spatula; cook until the other sides are golden brown and the patties are heated through, another 3 to 4 minutes.

½ pound halibut

2 tablespoons mayonnaise

1 egg

1 clove garlic, minced

Finely grated peel of 1 lemon

1 tablespoon freshly squeezed lemon juice

Pinch of freshly ground white pepper

Pinch of cayenne pepper

Pinch of freshly ground nutmeg

¼ cup heavy cream

1 pound crabmeat

1 teaspoon Old Bay seasoning

¼ teaspoon salt

Butter for frying

Dungeness Crab Mac and Cheese with Hazelnut Crust

SYBARIS, ALBANY, OR

4 SERVINGS

This takes comfort food to a new level! The flavor is awesome and the presentation is beautiful, especially if you opt to bake it in real crab shells (see variation). Either way, this is a delicious and fun way to enjoy Dungeness crabmeat.

1. Preheat the oven to 400°F. Cook the pasta in boiling water, following package directions, until it is not quite al dente. Drain and let cool.

2. In a medium saucepan, bring the cream to a boil over high heat. As soon as the cream boils, add the cooked pasta. Bring back to a boil and stir in the cheeses and mustard. Bring the mixture back to a boil and add the crabmeat, Tabasco, and salt. Remove from heat and season to taste with pepper.

3. Put the crab-pasta mixture in a greased casserole dish and sprinkle with the hazelnuts. Bake until hot and bubbly, 15 to 20 minutes.

Variation For an attractive presentation, bake the crab macaroni and cheese in clean crab shells. Ask your neighborhood fishmonger to save four crab shells for you to clean and bake in. Preheat the oven to 400°F. Place the shells on a baking sheet, carefully fill with the crab-pasta mixture, and sprinkle with the hazelnuts. Bake until hot and bubbly, 15 to 20 minutes.

2½ cups uncooked penne pasta

2 cups heavy cream

¼ cup grated Parmesan cheese

½ cup grated white cheddar cheese

1 tablespoon Dijon mustard

½ pound Dungeness crabmeat (from a 2-pound crab)

Dash of Tabasco

1 teaspoon salt

Freshly ground white pepper

½ cup hazelnuts, roasted and finely chopped

Lemon wedges (optional)

Crab Fettuccine with Wild Mushrooms

BAKED ALASKA, ASTORIA, OR

2 SERVINGS

Wild mushrooms add an earthy flavor and wonderful, contrasting texture to silky, slippery noodles and delicate crabmeat. Serve this dish with chilled wine, warm baguettes, and a simple salad of field greens, dried cranberries, and toasted pine nuts.

1. Cook the fettuccine according to package directions; keep warm. In a medium sauté pan, melt the clarified butter over medium heat. Sauté the mushrooms until brown and tender, 8 to 10 minutes, seasoning lightly with salt and pepper. Add the garlic; cook for 1 minute. Stir in the wine and saffron. Reduce the wine by half, 4 to 5 minutes.

2. Add the cream and swirl the pan until it is incorporated. Add the crab to the pan, and stir the mixture until the sauce reduces slightly. Season to taste with salt and pepper. Remove from the heat; add in the cold butter and stir until it is melted.

3. Toss the pasta with olive oil and a dash of salt and pepper. Place the pasta in individual bowls; top with the crab-mushroom sauce.

6 ounces fettuccine noodles

2 tablespoons clarified butter

4 ounces wild mushrooms (oyster, shiitake, or chanterelle), sliced

Salt and freshly ground black pepper

1 clove garlic, minced

½ cup dry white wine

Pinch saffron

¼ cup heavy cream

6 to 8 ounces fresh crabmeat

1 tablespoon cold butter

Olive oil

Garlic Shrimp Pasta

LONESOME COVE RESORT, FRIDAY HARBOR, WA   **2 SERVINGS**

Simple, fast, and everyone loves it! Add pepper flakes if you like it spicy, grated lemon peel if you like it tangy. Serve with an organic green salad or a steamed green vegetable like broccoli or snap peas. It's a perfect light summer pasta.

1. In large Dutch oven, heat 3 quarts water with 1 tablespoon of the olive oil and 1 tablespoon of the garlic salt; bring to a boil. Add the spaghetti and cook according to package directions. Drain the pasta and return to the Dutch oven to keep warm. Add 2 tablespoons of the olive oil and the Parmesan cheese; toss well.

2. Meanwhile, heat the remaining oil in a medium skillet over medium heat. Add the remaining garlic salt and minced garlic; cook for 1 minute. Add the shrimp; cook, stirring occasionally, until the shrimp turn pink, about 5 minutes.

3. To serve, toss the shrimp with the pasta. Add red pepper flakes and grated lemon peel to taste. Sprinkle with additional Parmesan and parsley. Garnish with lemon wedges. Serve warm.

¼ cup olive oil, divided

1 tablespoon plus 1 teaspoon garlic salt, divided

8 ounces spaghetti or other pasta of your choice

¼ cup grated Parmesan cheese, plus additional for serving

1 teaspoon freshly minced garlic

1 pound jumbo shrimp (16 to 20 per pound), peeled and deveined

Red pepper flakes (optional)

Grated lemon peel (optional)

Finely chopped parsley

Pan-Fried Oysters with Garlic Aioli

THE DEPOT RESTAURANT, SEAVIEW, WA

2 SERVINGS

There's nothing like hot, juicy pan-fried oysters—delicious with a squirt of lemon juice and hot sauce, and even better with this roasted garlic aioli. They're a treat to have for dinner with creamy coleslaw and corn on the cob. The aioli makes a great dipping sauce for steamed artichokes too!

1. Prepare the Garlic Aioli; reserve.

2. To prepare the oysters, combine the flour, garlic, salt, and pepper in a medium bowl. Drain the oysters; pat dry with paper towel. Dredge the oysters in the flour mixture. In a large skillet, heat 2 tablespoons of the reserved garlic olive oil (from preparing the Garlic Aioli) over high heat. Cook the oysters until golden brown on both sides, 2 to 3 minutes, adding more oil as necessary. Remove the oysters with a slotted spoon; drain on paper towels.

3. Serve the oysters immediately with the Garlic Aioli as a dipping sauce.

Garlic Aioli (recipe follows)

1 cup all-purpose flour

2 tablespoons granulated garlic

1 tablespoon kosher salt

½ teaspoon cayenne pepper

12 to 16 small to medium oysters

Garlic Aioli

In a small skillet, heat the olive oil over medium heat. Add the garlic cloves and sauté, stirring frequently, until golden brown. Remove the garlic cloves from the oil and set them aside to cool, reserving the oil for frying the oysters. When cool, put the garlic in a mini food processor or blender and purée. Add the mayonnaise, lemon juice, salt, and pepper; process until smooth.

¼ cup olive oil

8 whole garlic cloves

½ cup mayonnaise

2 tablespoons freshly squeezed lemon juice

¼ teaspoon kosher salt

¼ teaspoon freshly ground white pepper

Seared Scallops with Corn, Pancetta, and Green Onions

KING ESTATE WINERY, EUGENE, OR   **2 SERVINGS**

Large, succulent scallops surround a heap of creamy fresh corn, perfectly complemented by a rich, tangy balsamic sauce. This pairs nicely with a King Estate Domaine pinot gris.

1. Place the corn, green onions, and cream in a small saucepan and simmer until the mixture is thick and creamy; keep warm.

2. In a medium skillet, cook the pancetta over medium-high heat until it starts to get crispy. Season the scallops with salt and pepper; add to the pan with the bacon, leaving space between the scallops. Cook for 5 to 7 minutes, turning once, until the scallops are browned on both sides and opaque in the center.

3. To serve, spoon the corn mixture onto the center of each plate. Divide the scallops and place on top of the corn mixture. Spoon the Balsamic Sauce around the corn. Drizzle the olive oil around the Balsamic Sauce. Sprinkle with chives.

1 cup freshly shucked corn

4 green onions (green and pale green parts), chopped

½ cup heavy cream

1 ounce pancetta, diced

1 pound Alaskan sea scallops

Salt and freshly ground black pepper

Balsamic Sauce (recipe follows)

Olive oil (optional)

Snipped chives (optional)

Balsamic Sauce

In a small bowl, whisk together all the ingredients.

1 tablespoon balsamic vinegar

1 tablespoon soy sauce

1 tablespoon ketchup

1 tablespoon butter, melted

*Cranberry-Raspberry
Fruit Soup, page 3*

Balsamic Mushrooms and Brie Toast, page 34

Fresh Oysters with Tabasco and Lemongrass Granité, page 39

Warm Spring Salmon Salad, page 46

Chicken Roulade,
page 68

Dungeness Crab Mac and
Cheese with Hazelnut
Crust, page 78

Lavender Crème Brûlée,
page 110

Decadent Chocolate Mousse, page 114

Northwest Bouillabaisse

THE BLUE HERON INN, SECHELT, B.C.   **4 TO 6 SERVINGS**

Bouillabaisse has lots of ingredients, but don't be afraid to try it—you start with one pot and just keep adding to it, and the results are fantastic! The chef's tip is to employ the French technique of *mis en place,* having all the necessary ingredients for your dish prepared and ready before starting any cooking.

1. Combine 1 tablespoon of the oil with 1 minced garlic clove; let sit for at least 5 minutes. Grill or broil the baguette slices on one side. Brush the other side with the infused oil. Turn over and grill or broil until toasted; keep warm.

2. Heat the remaining oil over medium heat in a large sauté pan or Dutch oven; add the leek and onion and cook until translucent, 8 to 10 minutes. Add the remaining garlic and stir gently until it gives off its aroma. Add the stock, wine, tomato, fennel, bay leaf, and saffron; bring to a simmer. Submerge the mussels and clams in the stew. When the shellfish are just starting to open, add the cod, salmon, halibut, prawns, scallops, and crab. Once the prawns turn rosy pink, the stew is ready to serve. Season to taste with salt and pepper.

3. Serve in large bowls; sprinkle with fresh parsley and add a squeeze of lemon juice. Serve with the garlic baguette slices.

3 tablespoons olive oil, divided

3 garlic cloves, minced, divided

1 baguette, sliced on the diagonal

1 leek (white part only), minced

½ medium yellow onion, finely chopped

¾ cup vegetable stock

¼ cup dry white wine

1 plum tomato, peeled, seeded, and chopped

½ fennel bulb, thinly sliced

1 bay leaf

Pinch of saffron

12 mussels, scrubbed and debearded

12 clams, scrubbed

4 ounces each cod, salmon, and halibut

3 local prawns per person

3 local scallops per person

½ Dungeness crab per person, cooked

Salt and freshly ground black pepper

2 tablespoons chopped fresh parsley

2 lemons, quartered

Pasta Puttanesca with Ahi Tuna

SERAFINA OSTERIA & ENOTECA, SEATTLE, WA

2 SERVINGS

Puttanesca sauce is a spicy mélange of tomatoes, onions, capers, olives, anchovies, and garlic, originating in Naples. It's a relatively simple sauce to prepare, and it provides a palette of flavors that complements the ahi tuna in a most beautiful way.

1. Prepare the linguine according to package directions, until just al dente.

2. Heat 1 tablespoon of the oil over medium heat in a stainless steel saucepan. Add the onion; sauté until translucent, about 5 minutes. Add the garlic, pepper flakes, and saffron; sauté for 1 minute. Add the tomatoes, capers, anchovy paste, olives, and herbs; simmer for 15 minutes over medium-low heat. Season to taste with salt and pepper. Add the lemon zest just before tossing with the hot linguini.

3. Sprinkle the tuna lightly with salt and pepper. Heat the remaining olive oil in a sauté pan; sear the tuna until it reaches preferred doneness. (Note: At Serafina, a 1-inch-thick tuna steak is sautéed for 30 seconds on each side.) Cut the tuna into thin slices.

4. To serve, place the sauced pasta in individual bowls. Fan the sliced tuna over the pasta. Garnish with herb sprigs and lemon wedges.

6 ounces uncooked linguine

2 tablespoons olive oil, divided

½ cup diced yellow onion

3 cloves garlic, minced

Pinch or two of dried red pepper flakes

Pinch of saffron

1½ cups diced vine-ripened tomatoes

1 to 2 tablespoons capers, drained

1 tablespoon anchovy paste

½ cup chopped green olives

1 tablespoon chopped fresh Italian parsley

1 teaspoon chopped fresh oregano

1 teaspoon chopped fresh mint

Salt and freshly ground black pepper

1 tablespoon lemon zest

12 ounces ahi tuna

Fresh herb sprigs for garnish (optional)

Lemon wedges for garnish (optional)

Grilled Italian Tuna Steaks

COZY ROSE INN BED AND BREAKFAST, GRANDVIEW, WA

2 SERVINGS

It doesn't get much easier or tastier than this! The tuna is a delicious way of getting those omega-3 fatty acids. Serve it with a side dish of wild rice tossed with golden raisins and toasted slivered almonds, and a cool cucumber salad.

1. Place the tuna steaks in a shallow dish. Whisk the oil, vinegar, herbs, garlic, salt, and pepper in a small bowl. Pour this marinade over the steaks; turn to coat evenly. Let marinate for 30 to 45 minutes.

2. Preheat an outdoor grill. Lightly brush the grill rack with oil. Remove the tuna steaks from the marinade (reserve marinade); place on the grill. Cover and grill the steaks over medium heat for 5 minutes, brushing once with the reserved marinade. Turn the steaks; cook for 4 to 5 minutes or until the flesh flakes easily and the center is slightly pink.

2 tuna steaks, about ⅓ pound each

2 tablespoons olive oil plus additional for grilling

1 tablespoon white vinegar

1½ teaspoons crumbled dried oregano leaves

1 teaspoon crumbled dried thyme leaves

2 cloves garlic, minced

1 teaspoon salt

1 teaspoon ground black pepper

Alice Bay Barbecued Salmon

ALICE BAY BED & BREAKFAST, BOW, WA

6 SERVINGS

This is a simple and delicious way to serve salmon for a backyard barbecue on a summer evening in the Northwest. You may want to make up a double batch of the sauce to serve on the side—keep it separate from the basting sauce, though, to avoid cross-contamination.

1. In a small saucepan over medium heat, combine the butter, garlic, soy sauce, mustard, ketchup, and Worcestershire.

2. Preheat an outdoor grill. Lightly brush the grill rack with oil. Place the salmon on the grill over medium heat. Baste the salmon generously with the sauce. Grill just until the flesh flakes easily at the thickest part, about 10 minutes per 1-inch thickness.

3. Serve on a platter with lemon wedges.

½ cup (1 stick) butter

1 to 2 cloves garlic, minced

2 tablespoons soy sauce

1 tablespoon mustard

2 tablespoons ketchup

Dash of Worcestershire sauce

2 pounds wild salmon

Oil for grilling

Lemon wedges (optional)

Grilled Salmon with Raspberry and Tarragon Butter Sauce

MARKUS' WHARFSIDE RESTAURANT, SOOKE, B.C.

2 SERVINGS

This is a beautiful dish to serve when raspberries are in season. The rosy pink sauce has wine and fruit notes balanced with a sensuous butter-herb undertone. Wonderful served with grilled asparagus or arugula salad and a dry rosé.

1. Heat the oil in a medium saucepan over medium heat; add the shallot and cook until transparent, about 3 minutes. Add 1 cup of the raspberries and cook for about 1 minute. Add the wine and reduce the liquid by half, 4 to 5 minutes. Add the whipping cream and bring to a boil. Remove the pan from the heat. Add the butter one piece at a time, stirring until melted. Add the tarragon. Season to taste with salt and pepper. Set aside and keep warm.

2. Preheat an outdoor grill. Lightly brush the grill rack with oil. Grill the salmon fillets over medium-high heat for 10 to 12 minutes, turning once, until the flesh flakes easily with a fork.

3. To serve, place the salmon on a plate and drizzle the sauce around it. Garnish with the remaining raspberries.

1 tablespoon olive oil plus additional for grilling

1 shallot, finely chopped

1¼ cups fresh raspberries, divided

½ cup dry white wine

1 teaspoon whipping cream

¼ cup (½ stick) butter, cut into 4 pieces

1 sprig fresh tarragon leaves, finely chopped

Salt and freshly ground black pepper

2 salmon fillets, 6 to 7 ounces each

Halibut with Hazelnut Sauce

SILVERWATER CAFÉ, PORT TOWNSEND, WA

2 SERVINGS

This is an exquisite dish, evocative of the Pacific Northwest. Luscious hazelnut cream sauce meets succulent halibut and forms a perfect union that celebrates local bounty. Try this dish with halibut cheeks if you can find them.

1. Dust the halibut fillets with pepper. Heat the oil and butter over medium heat in a medium skillet. Add the halibut; cook until light golden brown, about 3 minutes. Turn the fillets; add the wine. Cover; cook until the wine is reduced to almost a glaze, about 10 minutes. Transfer the halibut to a serving platter and keep warm. Add the hazelnuts and salt to the skillet and stir to toast the nuts. Add the liqueur and reduce to a glaze. Add the cream and reduce to a thickened consistency.

2. To serve, pour the sauce over the halibut; sprinkle with toasted hazelnuts. Serve immediately.

Two 8-ounce halibut fillets

½ teaspoon freshly ground white pepper

½ tablespoon olive oil

½ tablespoon butter

½ cup dry white wine

2 tablespoons chopped hazelnuts

½ teaspoon salt

2 tablespoons hazelnut liqueur

½ cup heavy cream

2 tablespoons toasted chopped hazelnuts (optional)

Black Cod, Sweet Corn, and Fava Beans with Balsamic Brown Butter

CELILO RESTAURANT, HOOD RIVER, OR

4 SERVINGS

Prepare this dish from early to midsummer when fresh fava beans are available at your local farmers' market. Black cod is a rich, flavorful Pacific Coast fish with a delicate texture and flaky white flesh.

1. Remove the fava beans from their pods. Blanch the beans in salty boiling water for 2 minutes and transfer with a slotted spoon to a bowl of ice water (beans should be tender, but not mushy). Remove the beans from the ice water and peel off the outer skins. Set aside.

2. Shuck the corn from the cobs using a sharp knife, cutting no deeper then the midpoint of the kernels. Heat 2 tablespoons of the oil in a large skillet. When the oil just begins to smoke, add the corn. Stir frequently until the kernels have softened slightly, 3 to 4 minutes. Add the fava beans; stir until warm. Remove from the heat; stir in the tarragon. Season to taste with salt and pepper. Set aside.

3. To make the sauce, heat the butter over low heat in small saucepan and watch it carefully. When the butter starts to brown, remove the pan from the heat. Stir in the vinegar; set aside.

4. Cut the fish into four pieces, making them as uniform as possible. Pat the fish dry with a paper towel. Sprinkle both sides with salt and pepper. Heat a large skillet with the remaining oil. When the oil begins to smoke, gently add the fish. Sauté until a brown crust appears around the edge, 4 to 5 minutes. Gently turn the fish over and continue to cook for 4 to 5 minutes, or until the flesh turns opaque. Transfer to a paper towel.

5. To serve, spoon the corn-bean mixture in the centers of 4 plates. Place a piece of cod on top of the corn. Stir the sauce and drizzle it over the fish and onto the plate.

2 pounds whole fava beans in their pods

4 ears fresh sweet corn

4 tablespoons olive oil, divided

1 sprig fresh tarragon, leaves minced

Salt and freshly ground black pepper

2 tablespoons butter

2 tablespoons balsamic vinegar

1½ pounds whole black cod fillet, skinned and deboned

Pistachio-Crusted Sablefish with Roasted Red Pepper Sauce

QUATTRO AT WHISTLER, WHISTLER, B.C.

2 SERVINGS

Sablefish is another name for black cod—no matter the name, it's a luscious fish, boasting large flakes of buttery white meat. It is very high in healthy omega-3 fatty acids—about as much, ounce for ounce, as wild salmon.

1. Preheat the oven to 350°F. Coat the sablefish with oil; sprinkle with the garlic, salt, and pepper. Coat with the pistachios and place in a greased baking dish. Bake until the fish flakes easily with a fork, 10 to 20 minutes (depending on the thickness of the fish).

2. Serve the fish in a shallow pool of Roasted Red Pepper Sauce or drizzle the sauce on top of the fish.

¾ pound sablefish (black cod) or sea bass

2 teaspoons olive oil

½ teaspoon dried minced garlic

Salt and freshly ground black pepper

½ to ¾ cup pistachios, ground

Roasted Red Pepper Sauce (recipe follows)

Roasted Red Pepper Sauce

Heat the butter in a medium skillet over medium high heat. Add the shallot and cook for 2 minutes. Add the chopped peppers and sauté for 3 minutes. Add the stock and reduce by half, 4 to 5 minutes. Stir in the cream and honey and reduce to sauce consistency. Purée the sauce in a blender or food processor. Season to taste with salt and pepper. Add the basil.

Note: To make chiffonade, stack the basil leaves and roll up tightly, then cut into fine slices to create delicate shreds.

1 tablespoon butter

1 shallot, finely chopped

2 roasted red bell peppers, chopped

½ cup chicken or vegetable stock

¼ cup whipping cream

1 tablespoon honey

Salt and freshly ground black pepper

1 tablespoon fresh basil chiffonade (see Note)

Grilled Turkey Tenderloin with Sage Pesto

ABBEY ROAD FARM, CARLTON, OR

4 SERVINGS

A delicious treat any time of the year, this tenderloin is especially wonderful served in the fall with baked yams and roasted brussels sprouts. The sage pesto also makes a nice condiment with pork tenderloin. Serve it with a delicious local pinot noir.

Oil for grilling

Sage Pesto (recipe follows)

1 turkey tenderloin (or 2 turkey breast tenders), about 1½ pounds

1. Preheat an outdoor grill. Lightly brush the grill rack with oil. (To prepare this dish in the oven, preheat to 350° F, and bake the turkey in a covered baking pan for 30 minutes.) Rub a generous amount of the sage pesto on both sides of the turkey tenderloin; reserve the remaining pesto. Put the turkey on the grill over medium heat, cover, and grill for 30 minutes, turning after 15 minutes. The turkey is done when it is no longer pink in the center and the juices run clear.

2. Slice the tenderloin on the diagonal and serve with the remaining pesto on the side.

Sage Pesto

Put the sage, garlic, and walnuts in a food processor; process into a smooth paste. Add the cheese, salt, and pepper; pulse to mix well. With the food processor running, add the oil in a slow stream until it is completely incorporated and the pesto is the desired consistency.

One 1-ounce package fresh sage leaves

2 cloves garlic, peeled

½ cup roasted walnuts

½ cup freshly grated Parmigiano-Reggiano cheese

¾ teaspoon salt

¼ teaspoon freshly ground black pepper

⅓ cup olive oil

Pork Tenderloin with Caramelized Balsamic Onions

BLUE FJORD CABINS, LOPEZ ISLAND, WA

8 SERVINGS

The aroma alone will start you enjoying this succulent pork tenderloin covered with sweet caramelized onions. It's a perfect tummy-warmer for a cool, damp Pacific Northwest evening.

1. Wash the tenderloins; dry well with a paper towel. Heat the butter and 2 tablespoons of the oil in a heavy skillet over medium-high heat. Add the onions and cook for 10 to 15 minutes, stirring occasionally, until golden brown. Add the vinegar, sugar, salt, and pepper. Increase heat to high; stir for 2 minutes. Remove from heat.

2. Preheat the oven to 375° F. Rub the tenderloins with the remaining oil, salt, and pepper; let rest for 10 minutes. In a heavy skillet, lightly sear the tenderloins on all sides over high heat. Place the tenderloins in an oiled roasting pan and spoon the onion mixture over them. Cover and roast for about 30 minutes, or until the internal temperature of the pork is 150° F when measured with a meat thermometer. Remove from the oven; loosely cover to keep warm and let rest for 5 to 10 minutes.

3. To serve, cut the tenderloin across the grain into slices about ¾ inch thick. Spoon the onions and juices over the tenderloin slices.

2 pork tenderloins (1 to 1½ pounds each)

2 tablespoons butter

3 tablespoons olive oil, divided

3 large yellow onions, halved and thinly sliced

3 tablespoons balsamic vinegar

3 tablespoons packed brown sugar

¼ teaspoon salt

¼ teaspoon freshly ground pepper

Mama's Meatballs

THE PINK DOOR, SEATTLE, WA

4 SERVINGS

Those are *not* your ordinary meatballs! They are good enough to eat on their own, just the way they are. Wonderful herb and spice flavors explode in your mouth with every bite. Toss them with your own (or your mom's) spaghetti sauce to take them to a new level.

1. Preheat the oven to 375°F. In a medium bowl, combine the bread crumbs, egg, half-and-half, herbs, fennel seed, garlic, salt, and pepper. Add the ground beef; mix gently but thoroughly. Roll into 1½-inch meatballs and place on a baking pan. Bake until the meatballs are no longer pink in the center, 15 to 20 minutes.

5 tablespoons fresh bread crumbs

1 egg, lightly beaten

2 tablespoons half-and-half

5 tablespoons chopped fresh parsley

4 teaspoons dried basil

2 teaspoons dried oregano

2 teaspoons fennel seed

1 clove garlic, minced

½ teaspoon salt

½ teaspoon freshly ground black pepper

1 pound organic ground beef

Chateaubriand for Two

EL GAUCHO, SEATTLE, WA   **2 SERVINGS**

Chateaubriand is a small roast extravagantly cut from the center of the beef tenderloin. This cut is usually offered only as a serving for two.

1. Stir the butter and mustard together in a small bowl until smooth; set aside.

2. Preheat a grill. Lightly brush the grill rack with oil. Place the tenderloin on the hot grill and sear for 1 to 1½ minutes on each side. Reduce heat and continue grilling, turning occasionally, until the temperature reaches 120°F in the center (for medium rare) when measured with a meat thermometer. Remove the meat from the grill and place on a cutting board. Spread with the butter mixture.

3. Cut the meat into slices, being careful to reserve the drippings. Combine the red wine and Worcestershire sauce in a small bowl; stir in the meat drippings. Spoon the sauce over the slices.

2 tablespoons butter, softened

½ teaspoon Coleman's dry mustard

Oil for grilling

1 pound center-cut beef tenderloin

2 tablespoons cabernet sauvignon or merlot

1 teaspoon Worcestershire sauce

Pan-Seared Duck Breast with Roasted Tomato Relish

BRENTWOOD BAY LODGE & SPA, VICTORIA, B.C.

2 SERVINGS

There's an interesting Italian slant to this easy roasted duck dish. The duck meat itself is surpassingly tender, and the outside is deliciously crisp. And yes, it's OK to serve duck medium-rare (buy it from a trusted source, of course). Serve on a bed of wild rice or noodles with stir-fried broccoli on the side. Yum!

1. Preheat the oven to 400°F. Season both sides of the duck breasts with salt and pepper. Heat the oil in a large skillet over medium heat for 2 to 3 minutes, until almost smoking. Place the duck in the skillet, skin side down; sear for 3 to 4 minutes, until the skin is a rich golden brown. Turn the duck over; sear until golden brown, another 3 to 4 minutes. Transfer the duck to a baking sheet. Roast in the oven for 10 minutes (for medium-rare doneness). Allow the duck to cool for 3 minutes before slicing.

2. To serve, place 1 tablespoon of Roasted Tomato Relish on top of each breast.

2 duck breasts (boneless, skin-on)

½ teaspoon salt

½ teaspoon freshly ground black pepper

1 tablespoon canola oil

2 tablespoons Roasted Tomato Relish (recipe follows)

Roasted Tomato Relish

Preheat the oven to 400°F and grease a raised-edge baking sheet. Cut the tomatoes lengthwise into 4 to 6 wedges (depending on their size). Toss the tomatoes in the shallot, salt, pepper, and oregano, and roast on the baking sheet for 30 minutes; cool. Purée the tomatoes with the honey and vinegar in a food processor or blender.

6 plum tomatoes

1 shallot, finely minced

½ teaspoon salt

½ teaspoon pepper

1 teaspoon dried oregano

2 tablespoons honey

2 tablespoons sherry vinegar

Grilled Lamb Chops with Hazelnut Romesco Sauce

MARCHÉ, EUGENE, OR

4 SERVINGS

Here's a wonderful new take on grilled lamb—accompanied by Spanish romesco sauce, which traditionally includes almonds or hazelnuts, olive oil, garlic, onions, peppers, and/or tomatoes. Serve this with roasted or grilled veggies—both are wonderful with the sauce.

1. In a small bowl, combine the oil, thyme, rosemary, garlic, salt, and pepper. Rub mixture generously onto both sides of each lamb chop; cover and marinate in the refrigerator for at least 1 hour. Take the chops out of the refrigerator about 20 minutes before starting to grill.

2. Preheat an outside grill. Lightly brush the grill rack with oil. Grill the lamb chops over medium heat for 4 minutes. Turn the chops over and cook 2 to 3 minutes for medium rare, 4 to 5 minutes for medium; let sit for a few minutes before serving.

3. To serve, arrange two lamb chops artfully on each of 4 plates; drizzle with Hazelnut Romesco Sauce.

¼ cup olive oil plus additional for grilling

1 teaspoon chopped fresh thyme leaves

1 teaspoon finely chopped fresh rosemary

1 garlic clove, minced

¼ teaspoon salt

⅛ teaspoon freshly ground black pepper

Eight 1-inch-thick lamb chops

Hazelnut Romesco Sauce (recipe follows)

Hazelnut Romesco Sauce

In a food processor, combine the tomatoes, hazelnuts, vinegar, garlic, cayenne, paprika, and salt; purée until blended. Slowly add the oil. If the sauce is too thick, add water until the sauce attains desired pouring consistency.

½ cup peeled, seeded, and chopped fresh tomatoes or good-quality canned tomatoes, drained

⅓ cup hazelnuts

1 tablespoon red wine vinegar

1 garlic clove, minced

½ teaspoon cayenne pepper

½ teaspoon sweet smoked paprika

½ teaspoon salt

½ cup olive oil

Venison Tenderloin with Parsnip Purée and Blackberry Balsamic Gastrique

FREESTONE INN, MAZAMA, WA

4 SERVINGS

This is venison at its finest. First seared, then roasted with an exorbitantly flavorful rub, this venison is voluptuously set on a bed of silky puréed parsnips, then drizzled with a tangy, sweet blackberry balsamic reduction. This recipe is dedicated to one lucky wife whose husband (the chef) created a menu with all of her favorite ingredients. Now that's romance!

1. Preheat the oven to 350°F. Place the juniper berries, peppercorns, and fennel seeds in a baking pan; toast in the oven for 7 minutes. Grind the toasted spices in a spice grinder until fine. Rub the spice mixture over the venison loin and season with salt.

2. Increase the heat to 400°F. In a large skillet, sear the outside of the venison over high heat until browned on all sides. Place the venison in the oven for 8 minutes or until the internal temperature reaches at least 150°F (for medium rare) when measured with a meat thermometer. Let rest 10 minutes before carving.

3. To serve, mound the Parsnip Purée in the center of the plate. Fan the venison over the purée; spoon the Blackberry Balsamic Gastrique over and around the venison.

1 tablespoon juniper berries

1 tablespoon black peppercorns

1 teaspoon fennel seeds

1 to 1½ pounds venison tenderloin

Kosher salt

Parsnip Purée (recipe follows)

½ cup Blackberry Balsamic Gastrique (recipe follows)

Parsnip Purée

Put the parsnips in a large saucepan and cover with water. Simmer for 40 minutes, or until very tender; drain. Gently heat the cream and butter in a small saucepan until hot and melted. Transfer the parsnips and melted butter and cream to a food processor; purée until very smooth. Season to taste with salt.

2 pounds parsnips, peeled and chopped

¼ cup heavy cream

¼ cup (½ stick) butter

Salt

Blackberry Balsamic Gastrique

Heat the sugar in a small, heavy-bottomed saucepot over medium-high heat, stirring occasionally, until the sugar melts. Boil until the sugar turns a dark caramel color, stirring occasionally, about 5 minutes. Add the berries and stir vigorously. Remove from heat; add the vinegar and continue to stir vigorously (to prevent the mixture from seizing up in a solid mass). Reduce heat to low and simmer for 20 to 30 minutes, until the berries have softened and the caramelized sugar has dissolved. Allow the mixture to cool before transferring to a blender. Blend until smooth; strain. Season to taste with salt and pepper.

⅓ cup sugar

⅔ cup fresh or frozen (thawed) blackberries

¼ cup balsamic vinegar

Salt and freshly ground black pepper

Play It Softly

Music to dine by (and dance to):

Wild for You — Karrin Allyson

Something's Gotta Give (motion picture soundtrack)

When I Look in Your Eyes — Diana Krall

Music for Lovers — Joe Williams

Midnight in the Garden of Good and Evil (motion picture soundtrack)

It's Time — Michael Bublé

My Romance — Carly Simon

Come Away with Me — Norah Jones

Valentine — Jim Brickman

Moonglow — Sue Nixon and the Leo Raymundo Quartet

It Had to Be You — Rod Stewart

*"To love someone is to learn the song that is in that person's heart,
and to sing it to them when they have forgotten."*

—UNKNOWN SOURCE

·Desserts·

Pears Perfected	*Squalicum Lake Cottage*
Baked Apples à la Mode	*Lion and the Rose Victorian Bed & Breakfast*
Crème Fraîche Sorbetto with Balsamic-Pepper Strawberries	*Cafe Juanita*
Ice Wine Ice Cream with Roasted Rhubarb	*Trellis Restaurant*
Fromage de Coeur	*Hartmann House*
Zabaglione Tiramisu	*Taverna Tagaris*
Green Tea Crème Brûlée	*Dragonfly Bistro & Lounge*
Lavender Crème Brûlée	*Quails' Gate Estate Winery*
Molten Chocolate Cake with Cherry Sauce	*Harrison House Suites*
Decadent Chocolate Mousse	*Salish Lodge & Spa*
Chocolate Pavé	*Christina's Restaurant*
Chèvre Cheesecake with Fresh Berries	*Café Melange*
Pear and Almond Torte	*Duck Soup Inn*
White Chocolate Chunk and Pistachio Brownies	*Guest House Log Cottages*
Dutch Cookie Bars	*Turtleback Farm Inn*
Lemon Icebox Cookies	*Springbrook Hazelnut Farm Bed & Breakfast*
Country Inn Chocolate Chip Cookies	*Sandlake Country Inn*
Cranberry Oatmeal Chip Cookies	*Greenlake Guesthouse*
Port Truffles	*Fuse Waterfront Grill*
Fireside Coffee with Ultimate Whipped Cream	*FivePine Lodge*

Pears Perfected

SQUALICUM LAKE COTTAGE, BELLINGHAM, WA

2 SERVINGS

These pears are to die for! They're ideal if you're looking for a light and special dessert to serve after a heavy or rich meal. Garnish the finished pears with a cocoa-dusted chocolate cherry or a fresh mint leaf and an edible flower.

1. In a small bowl, mix the cream cheese, nuts, honey, and vanilla until well combined; set aside.

2. Pour 1 tablespoon of crème de cacao into the hollow of each pear half. Cover the pear halves loosely with plastic wrap and microwave until easily pierced with a knife, 2 to 3 minutes (depending on firmness). Pour off any remaining liquid.

3. Spoon half of the cream cheese mixture into the hollow of each pear half. Dust with cocoa. Serve immediately.

2 tablespoons cream cheese, at room temperature

1 tablespoon chopped walnuts or pecans

1 tablespoon honey

¼ teaspoon vanilla

2 tablespoons crème de cacao or brandy

1 fresh pear, halved and cored

1 tablespoon hot cocoa powder

Baked Apples à la Mode

LION AND THE ROSE VICTORIAN BED & BREAKFAST, PORTLAND, OR   **2 SERVINGS**

Perfect for a night at home when you need a little something sweet, but not too decadent. Cinnamon ice cream, if you can find it, is a real treat with this dessert.

1. Preheat the oven to 375° F. Grease a small baking dish or spray with cooking spray. Place the apple halves in the baking dish, cut side up.

2. In a small bowl, mix the melted butter, sugar, and vanilla. Brush the butter-sugar mixture over the apples. Sprinkle with additional brown sugar. Bake until the apples are soft and the tops are golden brown, 25 to 35 minutes.

3. Serve warm, topped with a scoop of ice cream and sprinkled with cinnamon.

1 large unpeeled Golden Delicious or other baking apple, halved and cored

2 tablespoons melted butter

1½ tablespoons brown sugar, plus additional for sprinkling (optional)

1 teaspoon vanilla

Vanilla ice cream

Ground cinnamon

Crème Fraîche Sorbetto with Balsamic-Pepper Strawberries

CAFE JUANITA, KIRKLAND, WA

4 SERVINGS

Even after a heavy meal, your guests will enjoy this refreshing sorbet. If you've never tried strawberries and balsamic vinegar together, you'll be amazed by this delightful combination.

1. Combine the cream, crème fraîche, water, sugar, and salt in a medium saucepan; simmer over low heat for 5 minutes, stirring occasionally. Cool completely, at least 4 hours but preferably overnight. Process the mixture in an ice cream maker according to manufacturer's instructions. For a harder sorbetto, freeze the ice cream mixture overnight.

2. In a medium bowl, toss the strawberries with the balsamic vinegar and pepper, coating the berries evenly. (Note: Wait until just before serving to complete this step to avoid the berries becoming mushy.) Serve the strawberries over the crème fraîche sorbetto. Garnish with a wafer cookie.

1 cup heavy cream

¾ cup crème fraîche

¾ cup water

¾ cup sugar

¼ teaspoon salt

2 cups sliced strawberries

1 tablespoon balsamic vinegar

⅛ teaspoon freshly cracked black pepper

Rolled wafer cookies (optional)

Ice Wine Ice Cream with Roasted Rhubarb and Strawberry Compote

TRELLIS RESTAURANT, KIRKLAND, WA

6 SERVINGS

Imagine summery, sweet, jammy fruit spooned over homemade vanilla bean ice cream infused with ice wine. This in itself could be a memorable occasion! To make vanilla sugar, bury a whole vanilla bean in a cup or two of sugar and leave it an airtight container for a week or two. Note that you'll need to start the ice cream one day in advance.

1. In a medium saucepan, bring the vanilla sugar, milk, cream, and salt to a simmer, stirring occasionally, until the sugar and salt have completely dissolved; strain through a fine mesh strainer. Chill in an ice bath. Place in the refrigerator overnight. The following day, stir in the ice wine. Process the chilled mixture in an ice cream maker according to the manufacturer's instructions.

2. Serve the ice cream topped with Roasted Rhubarb and Strawberry Compote.

1 cup vanilla sugar

1½ cups whole milk

3 cups heavy cream

⅛ teaspoon salt

¾ cup ice wine

Roasted Rhubarb and Strawberry Compote (recipe follows)

Roasted Rhubarb and Strawberry Compote

Preheat the oven to 350° F. Wash the rhubarb in cold water, then dry it well with paper towels. Trim both the leaf ends and the bottom of the stalks. Cut the stalks crosswise into ½-inch slices; put in a medium bowl. Add the orange juice, zest, and sugar; toss together. Put the mixture in a 9- or 10-inch nonaluminum baking pan. Cover with aluminum foil and bake for 25 minutes. Remove the foil and continue baking until the rhubarb is tender, 5 to 10 minutes (do not overbake). Let cool to room temperature. Add the strawberries to the rhubarb.

1 pound fresh rhubarb

4 tablespoons freshly squeezed orange juice

Zest from 1 orange

¾ cup sugar

½ pound fresh strawberries, hulled and quartered

Fromage de Coeur

4 SERVINGS

This creamy sweet cheese dessert is simple to prepare and requires no cooking. It does require you to have *coeur à la crème* molds, however. These sweet little white hearts, drizzled with raspberry purée, will surely win the heart of anyone they're presented to.

1. Wet four squares of double-thickness 100-percent-cotton cheesecloth. Squeeze out excess water. Line 4 *coeur à la crème* molds with the cheesecloth.

2. In a large bowl, whisk together the yogurt, ricotta, cream, sugar, and vanilla until thick. Spoon into the prepared molds, set them on a wire rack over a pan, refrigerate, and let stand and drain overnight.

3. In a blender, purée the raspberries until smooth. Strain through a sieve to remove the seeds. Taste for sweetness and add sugar if desired. Turn out the molded hearts onto individual plates. Pour the raspberry purée over the hearts (alternatively, spoon a pool of the sauce onto individual plates and place the molded hearts on top of the sauce); garnish with a sprig of mint and a few raspberries.

⅓ cup plain yogurt

1¼ cups ricotta cheese

⅓ cup whipping cream

2 tablespoons sugar, plus additional for berries (optional)

¼ teaspoon vanilla

1 cup fresh or frozen raspberries (thawed if frozen), plus additional for garnish

Fresh mint sprigs (optional)

Zabaglione Tiramisu

TAVERNA TAGARIS, RICHLAND, WA　　**6 SERVINGS**

This is an incredibly luscious, creamy, dreamy tiramisu . . . in a glass! Zabaglione is a traditional Italian custard made of egg yolks, sugar, and a sweet wine (usually marsala). This recipe calls for Kennedy port (a house blend of Gewürztraminer and Riesling produced at Tagaris Winery), but any late-harvest white or ice wine can be used in its place.

1. To make the zabaglione, combine the port, 4 of the egg yolks, and the sugar in a double boiler. Heat, whisking constantly, until the mixture reaches ribbon stage (it will be light and fluffy, like whipped custard), about 5 minutes; remove from heat. Chill in the refrigerator for at least 30 minutes.

2. Using an electric mixer, beat the mascarpone and remaining egg yolk in a large bowl until well combined. Chill in the refrigerator.

3. When ready to serve, fold the zabaglione into the mascarpone mixture. In a medium bowl, beat the cream, sugar, and vanilla until stiff peaks form; fold the whipped cream into the zabaglione-mascarpone mixture.

4. To assemble, pour 2 tablespoons of chocolate sauce into the bottom of each of 6 stemmed glasses; top each with a generous ½ cup of the zabaglione-mascarpone mixture. Place the glasses on small plates. Place a ladyfinger on each plate. Garnish with chocolate shavings. Serve a shot of espresso alongside the zabaglione.

½ cup Kennedy port or late-harvest white wine

5 egg yolks, divided

4 tablespoons sugar

6 ounces mascarpone cheese

¾ cup whipping cream

6 tablespoons powdered sugar

1 teaspoon vanilla

¾ cup chocolate sauce or chocolate-espresso dip

6 ladyfingers

Chocolate shavings (optional)

6 shots of espresso (optional)

Green Tea Crème Brûlée

DRAGONFLY BISTRO & LOUNGE, LEAVENWORTH, WA

6 SERVINGS

Y ou will see why this is described as heaven when your spoon cracks through the toasted sugar crust to expose a pool of pale green silk. The mild green tea flavor permeating the vanilla custard makes it interesting, but it's not at all bitter. Note that the baked custards must be refrigerated for at least four hours before completing the brûlée topping and serving.

3 cups heavy whipping cream

1 cup whole milk

¼ cup loose green tea leaves

1 vanilla bean

8 egg yolks

½ cup granulated sugar

Dash kosher salt

12 teaspoons turbinado or granulated sugar, for brûlée topping, divided

1. Preheat the oven to 300°F. Place six 6-ounce ceramic ramekins in a baking pan (2 to 3 inches deep). In a medium saucepan, heat the cream, milk, tea leaves, vanilla bean seeds (split pod and carefully scrape seeds out of pod), and vanilla bean pod, until a few bubbles rise to the surface (just before liquid begins to boil). Remove from heat and let steep for 15 minutes. Remove vanilla pod. Strain the cream mixture through a fine mesh strainer; discard the tea leaves and vanilla bean seeds.

2. In a separate medium bowl, whisk the egg yolks, sugar, and salt together until all the sugar has dissolved and the mixture is pale yellow. Add ½ cup of the cream mixture to the egg yolks while whisking constantly. Slowly add the remaining cream mixture, while continuing to whisk. After all the ingredients have been combined, strain the liquid again to remove any solids that may have formed.

3. Pour the custard mixture into the ramekins. Place the ramekins in the baking pan and fill the pan with water around the ramekins, up to the level of the cream mixture. Bake until set but still jiggly, 30 to 35 minutes. Cool to room temperature, then refrigerate uncovered for at least 4 hours. (If chilling overnight, cover each ramekin tightly with plastic wrap. These will keep for 2 to 3 days.)

4. When ready to serve, sprinkle 2 teaspoons sugar over the surface of each custard. Caramelize with a kitchen torch, moving the flame continuously over the sugar in a circular motion until the sugar is melted and light golden brown. Serve immediately.

Ten Romantic Movie Classics

The Philadelphia Story, 1940 (Katharine Hepburn, Cary Grant, James Stewart)
Casablanca, 1942 (Ingrid Bergman, Humphrey Bogart)
Adam's Rib, 1949 (Katharine Hepburn, Spencer Tracy)
The African Queen, 1951 (Katharine Hepburn, Humphrey Bogart)
Roman Holiday, 1953 (Audrey Hepburn, Gregory Peck)
Sabrina, 1954 (Audrey Hepburn, William Holden, Humphrey Bogart)
An Affair to Remember, 1957 (Deborah Kerr, Cary Grant)
Pillow Talk, 1959 (Doris Day, Rock Hudson)
Breakfast at Tiffany's, 1961 (Audrey Hepburn, George Peppard)
Doctor Zhivago, 1965 (Julie Christie, Omar Sharif)

"Like a perfect scene, from a movie screen, we're a dream come true,
suited perfectly, for eternity, me and you."

—KENNY CHESNEY

Lavender Crème Brûlée

QUAILS' GATE ESTATE WINERY, KELOWNA, B.C.

8 SERVINGS

This is great for serving at a dinner party. Light but rich, each crème brûlée is garnished with a fresh lavender sprig to add to its elegance. The term *culinary lavender* usually refers to English lavender, which has a sweeter, more delicate fragrance than French lavender. Note that the baked custards must be refrigerated for at least three hours or preferably overnight before completing the brûlée topping and serving.

4 cups heavy whipping cream

1 teaspoon dried culinary lavender

12 large egg yolks

1 cup plus 16 teaspoons granulated sugar, divided

1. In a large, heavy saucepan over medium heat, heat the cream and lavender just to a simmer. Remove from heat; allow lavender to infuse with the cream for 1 hour. Strain the cream mixture through a fine mesh strainer; discard the lavender.

2. Preheat the oven to 300°F. In a large bowl, whisk together the egg yolks and 1 cup of the sugar until light and creamy. Slowly add the cream mixture to the egg yolks while whisking constantly.

3. Strain the mixture to remove any foam that has formed on top. Ladle the mixture into eight 6-ounce ramekins. Place the ramekins in a roasting pan; fill the pan with water around the ramekins, up to the level of the cream mixture. Cover with foil, but leave an opening at one end of the pan to vent steam. Bake for 1 hour, or until the sides of the custards are firm but the centers are still fairly soft.

4. Remove the ramekins from the pan; let cool. Chill in the refrigerator for at least 3 hours or preferably overnight. (If chilling overnight, cover each ramekin tightly with plastic wrap. These will keep for 2 to 3 days.)

5. To serve, sprinkle 2 teaspoons sugar over the surface of each custard. Caramelize the sugar using a kitchen torch, moving the flame continuously over the sugar in a circular motion until the sugar is melted and light golden brown. Serve immediately.

Molten Chocolate Cake with Cherry Sauce

HARRISON HOUSE SUITES, FRIDAY HARBOR, WA

6 SERVINGS

This dessert is definitely for the chocolate lover (or lovers). The cake itself looks innocent at first glance—it's not until your spoon dives through the surface and into a pool of intense puddinglike decadence that its true character is revealed.

1. Preheat the oven to 300° F. In a medium saucepan, bring ½ cup of the sugar and the water almost to a boil. Remove from heat; stir in the chocolate and butter until combined and thoroughly melted.

2. In a large mixing bowl, combine the remaining sugar and the eggs; beat until the mixture forms ribbons when dropped from the spoon, 4 to 5 minutes. Fold into the chocolate mixture until just combined, being careful not to overmix.

3. Grease six 6-ounce ramekins and fill three-quarters full with chocolate mixture. (The batter can be refrigerated at this point and baked close to serving time, allowing 30 minutes for the cakes to cool.)

4. Place the ramekins in a roasting pan and carefully fill the pan with *hot* water halfway up the sides of the ramekins. Bake until a toothpick inserted in the center comes out with a few fine crumbs, 30 to 35 minutes. Let cool to room temperature, about 30 minutes. Meanwhile, prepare the Chocolate Ganache and Cherry Sauce.

5. To serve, drizzle Chocolate Ganache over the cakes. Serve with warm Cherry Sauce and whipped cream.

½ cup plus 1½ tablespoons sugar, divided

⅓ cup water

6½ ounces good-quality bittersweet chocolate, roughly chopped

½ cup (1 stick) plus 1 tablespoon butter, cut into 1-tablespoon pieces

3 large eggs, at room temperature

Chocolate Ganache (recipe follows)

Cherry Sauce (recipe follows)

Whipped cream (optional)

Chocolate Ganache

Bring the cream to a simmer; remove from heat. Stir in the chocolate until melted. Let stand for about 5 minutes or until the ganache mounds slightly when dropped from a spoon.

½ cup heavy cream

3 ounces bittersweet chocolate, coarsely chopped

Cherry Sauce

Combine the cherries (with juice), sugar, liqueur, and cinnamon in a heavy medium saucepan. Stir over medium heat until the sugar dissolves. Simmer until the sauce thickens and is slightly reduced, about 10 minutes. Serve warm.

One 12-ounce bag frozen pitted dark sweet cherries, thawed

½ cup sugar

¼ cup cherry liqueur or Chambord liqueur

¼ teaspoon cinnamon

Decadent Chocolate Mousse

SALISH LODGE & SPA, SNOQUALMIE, WA

8 SERVINGS

This is a great company dessert because it looks elegant, everyone loves chocolate, and you can make it ahead. Think of fun ways to serve it—funky tea cups, martini glasses, or long-stemmed wine glasses with iced tea spoons!

12 ounces semisweet chocolate, broken into 1-inch pieces

2¾ cups heavy cream

3 eggs, at room temperature

2 egg yolks, at room temperature

½ cup sugar

Whipped cream for garnish (optional)

Fresh raspberries (optional)

Chocolate curls (optional)

1. Melt the chocolate in a double boiler; set aside. In a separate bowl, whip the cream to medium stiff peaks; set aside.

2. In a large stainless steel bowl, combine the eggs, egg yolks, and sugar. Place the bowl over a hot water bath and whisk until the mixture reaches 140°F; remove from heat. With an electric mixer, whip the heated mixture on high speed until cool, about 3 minutes. Whisk in the melted chocolate. Gently fold in the whipped cream. Pour the mousse into 8 individual serving cups (about 5 ounces). Chill until set, about 1 hour.

3. To serve, garnish with a dollop of whipped cream, raspberries, or chocolate curls.

Long Kiss Goodnight Martini

Shake up two of these martinis or share sips of one—between kisses!

½ ounce vanilla vodka
1 ounce vodka
½ ounce white crème de cacao

Freeze a martini glass with finely shaved chocolate on the rim. Shake all ingredients in a shaker with ice. Pour into the martini glass. Garnish with a chocolate kiss.

Chocolate Pavé

CHRISTINA'S RESTAURANT, EASTSOUND, WA   **8 SERVINGS**

This recipe appears in *Christina's Cookbook* and it is truly for the serious chocolate lover: dangerous, sinful, and definitely worth every bite!

1. Melt the chocolate with the espresso and cream in a double boiler. Meanwhile, line a 4½- by 8½-inch loaf pan with plastic wrap, allowing extra wrap to drape over the sides. When the chocolate is thoroughly melted, remove it from the heat and whisk in the butter and Frangelico. Pour the chocolate mixture into the loaf pan and finish by smoothing the top. Tap the pan on the counter a few times to settle the contents. Fold the extra plastic wrap carefully over the top of the chocolate mixture. Chill for at least 6 hours or overnight.

2. To serve, remove the chilled pavé from the refrigerator; let sit at room temperature for 5 minutes. Gently lift the edge of the plastic wrap to remove the pavé from the pan. Unwrap and cut the pavé into thick slices with a warm knife. Serve at room temperature with Fresh Raspberry Sauce ladled around it.

14 ounces bittersweet chocolate, broken into 1-inch pieces

2 tablespoons espresso or strong coffee

½ cup heavy cream

½ cup (1 stick) butter, at room temperature

¼ cup Frangelico hazelnut liqueur

Fresh Raspberry Sauce (recipe follows)

Fresh Raspberry Sauce

Purée the raspberries, vinegar, sugar, and water in a food processor or blender. Add more sugar to taste if needed. Press the purée through a fine-mesh strainer to remove any seeds. Keep chilled. (Note: The sauce refrigerates well for about 24 hours, but it may begin separating if stored any longer. It will freeze well if sealed in an airtight container and wrapped.)

One 12-ounce bag frozen raspberries, thawed and drained

1 tablespoon balsamic vinegar

½ cup sugar

¾ cup water

Chèvre Cheesecake with Fresh Berries

CAFÉ MELANGE, YAKIMA, WA — **16 SERVINGS**

Here's a wonderful, rich, and creamy twist on the classic cheese-cake. Thick slabs are served with a mélange of fresh berries. It's equally delicious with a drizzle of raspberry coulis or made with a gingersnap or graham cracker crust.

*One-and-a-half
7-ounce packages
ladyfinger cookies*

*1¾ cups plus
2 teaspoons sugar,
divided*

*4 tablespoons butter,
melted*

*1½ pounds soft goat
cheese (chèvre)*

*Two 8-ounce packages
cream cheese*

1 teaspoon vanilla

4 eggs

Assorted fresh berries

1. Preheat the oven to 400° F. In a food processor, combine the cookies and 2 teaspoons of the sugar; pulse until reduced to fine crumbs. In a medium bowl, combine the melted butter and the crumbs; mix with a fork. Put the mixture into a 10-inch springform pan and press it over the bottom and up the edges with the back of a spoon. Bake the crust until golden brown, 8 to 10 minutes. Remove from the oven, leaving the heat at 400° F. Allow the crust to cool slightly before filling.

2. In a food processor or in a medium bowl with an electric mixer, combine the cheeses; process until blended and creamy. Add the remaining sugar and vanilla; process until well blended. Add the eggs, one at a time, processing after each addition. Pour into the crust; use a spatula to smooth the top.

3. Wrap the springform pan in two layers of foil. Place the pan in a hot water bath with 1 inch of water around the sides. Bake for 10 minutes. Turn the oven down to 325° F. Continue baking until the top is light golden and firm to the touch, 40 to 50 minutes. Let cool completely before serving, at least 2 to 3 hours, or refrigerate overnight.

4. Serve the cheesecake topped with fresh berries.

Pear and Almond Torte

10 SERVINGS

Cozy up to a slice of this rich and earthy pear torte. It is scrumptious! Almond paste (found in the baking section of most grocery stores) imparts a rich nutty flavor as well as a moist, chewy texture to baked goods.

1. Preheat the oven to 350° F. Liberally butter a 10-inch springform pan; coat with cookie crumbs. Sprinkle ½ cup of the sliced almonds evenly over the bottom of the pan.

2. In a blender or food processor fitted with a steel blade, process the sugar and almond paste until mostly lump free. In a medium bowl, cream together the sugar-almond mixture and butter. Add the eggs and vanilla; mix thoroughly.

3. In a separate bowl, combine the flour, baking powder, salt, and rosemary. Add the dry ingredients to the butter mixture and gently stir until thoroughly mixed. Spoon the batter carefully over the almonds in the pan; spread evenly. Sprinkle the diced pear over the batter; sprinkle with the remaining sliced almonds. Sprinkle the lemon juice liberally over the torte; sprinkle with sugar. Bake for 45 minutes, or until the torte is golden brown and a toothpick inserted in the center comes out clean. Cool slightly. Remove the sides of the pan.

4. Serve warm in wedges, with a dollop of crème fraîche.

Butter for coating pan

2 to 3 tablespoons sugar cookie crumbs or fine bread crumbs

1½ cups sliced almonds, divided

1 cup sugar

2 tablespoons canned almond paste

¼ cup (½ stick) butter, softened

2 eggs

2 teaspoons vanilla

1 cup all-purpose flour

1½ teaspoons baking powder

½ teaspoon salt

¼ teaspoon chopped fresh rosemary

2 to 3 ripe Bosc pears, peeled and diced (about 2 cups)

Freshly squeezed lemon juice

1 tablespoon turbinado or granulated sugar

Crème fraîche or whipped cream (optional)

White Chocolate Chunk and Pistachio Brownies

GUEST HOUSE LOG COTTAGES, GREENBANK, WA

16 BROWNIES

These are very moist, cakey brownies with an intense deep-chocolate flavor; they are not overly sweet. If you have an insatiable sweet tooth, you may want to frost them with chocolate or vanilla buttercream frosting. They freeze well, but don't plan on having many left over!

1. Preheat the oven to 350° F. Spread the pistachios on a raised-edge baking sheet and toast for 7 minutes. Cool slightly, then coarsely chop; set aside.

2. Grease a 9-inch-square baking pan or spray with cooking spray. In a large bowl, cream together the butter and brown sugar. Stir in the oil, eggs, and vanilla; mix well. Melt the semisweet chocolate in a double boiler or in a microwave at 50 percent power for 1 to 4 minutes, stirring every 30 seconds, until melted. Let cool slightly, then pour gradually into the batter, stirring until well combined. Stir in the flour, cocoa powder, and baking powder. Stir in the pistachios and white chocolate.

3. Pour the batter into the greased pan and spread evenly. Bake until a toothpick inserted in the center comes out clean, 40 to 45 minutes. Cool slightly before cutting.

¾ cup shelled pistachios

½ cup (1 stick) butter, softened

1 cup packed brown sugar

⅓ cup vegetable oil

3 eggs, lightly beaten

1 teaspoon vanilla

8 ounces semisweet chocolate, coarsely chopped

⅓ cup all-purpose flour

2 tablespoons cocoa powder

½ teaspoon baking powder

4 ounces white chocolate, coarsely chopped

Dutch Cookie Bars

48 BARS

This is Dutch shortbread at its finest. Not only do these bars smell good (think butter and cinnamon) when they're baking, but they taste incredible (you will savor one after another!). They pack and freeze well too.

1. Preheat the oven to 350°F. Grease a 10- by 15- by 1-inch baking pan or spray with cooking spray. In a food processor or in a medium bowl using an electric mixer, cream together the butter, shortening, sugar, and egg yolk. Add the flour, cinnamon, vanilla, and salt; pulse until blended.

2. Press the dough evenly into the baking pan. Brush the top with the egg white; sprinkle with almonds. Bake until a toothpick inserted in the center comes out clean, 20 to 25 minutes. Cool for 5 minutes before cutting into bars. Transfer the bars to a wire rack and let cool completely.

½ cup (1 stick) butter, softened

½ cup vegetable shortening

1 cup sugar

1 egg yolk

2 cups all-purpose flour

1 teaspoon cinnamon

½ teaspoon vanilla

¼ teaspoon salt

1 egg white, slightly beaten

1 cup sliced almonds or pecans

Lemon Icebox Cookies

SPRINGBROOK HAZELNUT FARM BED & BREAKFAST, NEWBERG, OR

3 DOZEN COOKIES

Serve these refreshingly lemony cookies with fresh raspberries at breakfast or with a glass of *limoncello* after dinner. Tender and sweet — what could be more romantic?

1. Line an empty waxed paper box with waxed paper. In a large bowl, cream together the shortening, butter, and sugar until light and fluffy. Stir in the lemon zest, juice, and extract. Mix the flour, baking powder, baking soda, and salt in a medium bowl; stir into the creamed mixture until well combined.

2. Press the dough into the lined box, making a squared roll the length of the box. (Alternatively, roll the dough in a sheet of waxed paper to form a log approximately 1½ inches in diameter) Place in the freezer until firm, about 2 hours.

3. Preheat the oven to 350° F. With a very sharp knife, cut the dough into thin slices, about ¼ inch thick; place on an ungreased cookie sheet, about 2 inches apart (the cookies will spread). Bake until the edges begin to turn light brown, 10 to 12 minutes. Cool on a wire rack. With a pastry brush, brush the cookies with Lemon Glaze; sprinkle with lemon zest.

½ cup vegetable shortening

3 tablespoons butter

1 cup sugar

Zest of 2 lemons, plus additional for topping (optional)

¼ cup freshly squeezed lemon juice

Few drops lemon extract or lemon oil

1¾ cups all-purpose flour

1½ teaspoons baking powder

¼ teaspoon baking soda

¼ teaspoon salt

Lemon Glaze (recipe follows)

Lemon Glaze

In a small bowl, stir the juice into the sugar, a tablespoon at a time, until the consistency is smooth and spreadable.

1 cup powdered sugar

2 to 3 tablespoons freshly squeezed lemon juice

Country Inn Chocolate Chip Cookies

SANDLAKE COUNTRY INN, PACIFIC CITY, OR

4 DOZEN COOKIES

Moist and chewy, these chocolate chip cookies have a hint of cinnamon. All you need to add is a glass of cold milk!

1. In a large bowl, cream together the butter and brown sugar. Add the egg and vanilla; beat until the mixture is light and fluffy, about 5 minutes. In a medium bowl, combine the flour, ginger, cinnamon, baking soda, and salt. Add this mixture to the butter mixture; stir until well blended. Add the chocolate chips and walnuts. Cover the dough and refrigerate for at least 4 hours or overnight. (You can refrigerate the dough for up to 2 weeks.)

2. To bake, preheat the oven to 350°F. Form the dough into 1-inch balls. Place a small amount of powdered sugar in a resealable bag; place several balls in the bag and shake to evenly coat. Place on an ungreased cookie sheet about 2 inches apart. Bake until golden brown, 10 to 12 minutes. Cool for 2 to 3 minutes on the sheet; transfer to a wire rack.

1 cup (2 sticks) butter, softened

1½ cups packed brown sugar

1 egg

1 teaspoon vanilla

2 cups all-purpose flour

1 teaspoon ground ginger

½ tablespoon ground cinnamon

1 teaspoon baking soda

½ teaspoon salt

1½ cups chocolate chips

1 cup finely chopped walnuts

Powdered sugar

Cranberry Oatmeal Chip Cookies

GREENLAKE GUESTHOUSE, SEATTLE, WA

4 DOZEN COOKIES

These cookies will quickly become a year-round favorite, but they are especially popular around the holidays. Make them with white chocolate chips for the festive parties or extra-large chocolate chunks for more decadence!

1. Preheat the oven to 350°F. In a large bowl, beat together the butter and both sugars until creamy. Add the eggs and vanilla; beat well. In a medium bowl, combine the flour, cinnamon, baking soda, and salt. Add the dry ingredients to the butter-sugar mixture and mix until well combined. Stir in the oats, cranberries, and chocolate chips.

2. Drop the dough by rounded tablespoonfuls onto an ungreased cookie sheet, about 2 inches apart. Bake until golden brown, 8 to 10 minutes. Cool for 1 minute on the cookie sheet; transfer to a wire rack. (Note: To make larger cookies, use a small muffin scoop to measure, and bake about 5 minutes longer.)

1 cup (2 sticks) butter, softened

1 cup packed brown sugar

½ cup sugar

2 eggs

1 teaspoon vanilla

1½ cups all-purpose flour

1 teaspoon ground cinnamon

1 teaspoon baking soda

½ teaspoon salt

3 cups oats (quick or rolled)

1 cup dried cranberries

2 cups semisweet chocolate or white chocolate chips

Port Truffles

FUSE WATERFRONT GRILL, SOOKE, B.C.

24 TRUFFLES

If you are looking for the quintessential experience of decadent chocolate, look no further! Not only are these truffles easy to make, they are also wonderfully easy to indulge in. For your own sake (and that of your waistline), you may want to give these away . . . and quickly!

¾ cup heavy whipping cream

10 ounces dark chocolate, coarsely chopped

1 ounce port

¼ cup cocoa powder

1. In a medium saucepan, heat the cream until just below simmering. Add the chocolate and stir until completely melted. Stir in the port. Cool to room temperature. Whisk for 1 minute. Refrigerate until the chocolate hardens, 45 to 60 minutes. Using your hands (or a melon baller), form 2-teaspoon portions of the mixture into balls. Place the truffles on a baking sheet covered with parchment paper. Freeze for 30 minutes.

2. Place the cocoa in a small bowl; gently roll the truffles in the cocoa until they are evenly coated. Store the truffles in the refrigerator in an airtight container, layered with wax paper.

Fireside Coffee with Ultimate Whipped Cream

2 SERVINGS

This is for one of those chilly "sit in front of the fire and be happy you're home" sort of nights. You'll have some of the whipped cream left over, so you'll need to use your imagination for what to do with the rest. *Bon appétit!*

1. Rub the rims of two heat-resistant glass mugs with a lemon wedge; dip the rims in sugar. Add 1½ ounces of the Bacardi rum to each glass and *very carefully* light the rum on fire with a long-handled match. Rotate the glass in a complete circle very slowly so the heat of the flaming rum caramelizes the sugar on the rim. After caramelizing the sugar, add 1½ ounces of the Tia Maria to each glass. Pour 1½ cups of coffee into each glass. Serve with a dollop of Ultimate Whipped Cream.

Lemon wedge

Granulated sugar

3 ounces Bacardi 151 rum, divided

3 ounces Tia Maria liqueur, divided

3 cups hot coffee (your favorite blend), divided

Ultimate Whipped Cream (recipe follows)

Ultimate Whipped Cream

In a small bowl, beat the whipping cream with the powdered sugar and the vanilla bean seeds. Continue to whip at medium speed until stiff peaks begin to form, about 7 minutes. Gently stir in the Grand Marnier and serve immediately.

1 cup heavy whipping cream

½ cup powdered sugar

Seeds from ½ vanilla bean

¼ cup Grand Marnier liqueur

Chocolate Dip for Two

Serve this after a special dinner or a night out on the town. Pick one or two dippers from the list below or use your imagination and come up with your own!

Fondue:

½ cup heavy cream

8 ounces semisweet chocolate, chopped

1 tablespoon amaretto, Frangelico, or Kahlúa

Directions:

Bring the cream to a simmer in a small saucepan; remove from heat. Stir in the chocolate until it is melted. Stir in the liqueur. Transfer mixture to a small fondue pot and keep warm.

Treats for dipping:

Dried mangos and apricots

Spears of fresh pineapple

Whole strawberries

Fresh cherries

Banana bread

Marshmallows

Pound cake

Biscotti

Pretzels

Oreos

Fingers

"All I really need is love, but a little chocolate now and then doesn't hurt!"

—LUCY (FROM *PEANUTS*)

Review Appendix

ROMANTIC LODGING

Abbey Road Farm

10501 NE Abbey Rd, Carlton, OR; 503/852-6278

Perched atop a hill overlooking acres of country landscapes, this working farm and bed-and-breakfast offers breathtaking views, as well as a spirit of adventure for guests: each of the five circular suites is located in a refurbished silo. These insulated spaces are the perfect secluded places for a peaceful country weekend. Modern amenities include Jacuzzi tubs, heated towel racks, Egyptian cotton sheets, in-room CD players, and a king-size bed in all but one room. In the fall, golden fields outside echo the Tuscan hues of the silo interiors. In spring, the farm's cherry orchard is in full bloom, providing a bud-covered walking path for twitterpated couples. Guests can pick fresh tomatoes and grapes from the spacious garden and enjoy an impromptu picnic here or on one of two decks overlooking the valley. *$$$; AE, MC, V; checks OK; www.abbeyroad farm.com.*

The Aerie Resort & Spa

600 Ebedora Ln, Malahat, B.C.; 250/743-7115 or 800/518-1933

A beautiful half-hour drive from Victoria leads to this grandiose faux-Mediterranean villa complex with spectacular views of the distant Olympic Mountains, tree-covered hills, and peaceful fjords below. While the famously opulent interior may overwhelm those with simpler tastes, choose among the 35 rooms and suites to find one that fits your style; most offer tubs for two, private decks, and fireplaces. Romantics seeking the ultimate in luxury, privacy, and scenery may opt for one of the six suites in the separate two-story Villa Cielo, enjoying terraced gardens, a reproduction of Michelangelo's *David*, and expansive views of Finlayson Arm and distant mountains. Guests have access to the resort's facilities, including three kiss-worthy spots: an outdoor hot tub with a view, a beautiful glass-enclosed pool, and a luxurious spa. A complimentary full breakfast is served in the elegant dining room overlooking the inspiring mountain scenery. Lunch and dinner are also available to both guests and nonguests. *$$$$; AE, DC, MC, V; no checks; www.aerie.bc.ca.*

Alice Bay Bed & Breakfast

11794 Scott Rd, Samish Island, Bow, WA; 360/766-6396

Burgeoning naturalists who make the trip to Alice Bay B&B—located outside of La Conner on quiet Samish Island—may just proclaim it their personal wonderland by the end of their stay. Alice Bay is home to a great blue heron rookery, but couples strolling along the private beach may be lucky enough to also spot the area's resident bald eagles, hawks, and falcons. As for the guest quarters, which are separated from the owners' house by a breezeway, the modest but comfortable setup includes a queen bed, a serene view of the bay, and thick, cozy robes—to keep you warm on the journey to the outdoor hot tub. As you are the only guests on the premises, a sumptuous breakfast is delivered to your door at the time you specify. Do your best to wake up with a healthy appetite for signature Alice Bay French Toast or a Grand Dutch Baby. Because of popular demand, the *Alice Bay Cookbook* of favorite recipes has been compiled including these two specialties. *$$$; AE, DIS, MC, V; checks OK; www.alicebay.com.*

Ann Starrett Mansion

744 Clay St, Port Townsend, WA; 360/385-3205 or 800/321-0644

Port Townsend's grand past has been beautifully and authentically revived in this ornate 1889 Victorian home set on a scenic bluff that's just a two-minute walk from downtown. A Gothic octagonal tower is the focal point of the mansion, and rich red-and-green-gabled detailing adorns the exterior. Inside, a free-hung, three-tiered circular staircase spirals up the tower. Be sure to stop and gaze at the eight-sided dome ceiling, where frescoes depict the four seasons and the four cardinal virtues. Every aspect of this inn's classic Victorian elegance will embrace you in stunning splendor. All nine guest rooms offer rich color schemes, original period furnishings, antique brass and canopied beds, and lace curtains. Next door, the Starrett Cottage holds a pair of two-room suites, which, although not quite as grand as those in the main house, are both private and spacious. It won't be easy to leave these gorgeous rooms, but trust us, the award-winning full gourmet breakfast, served in the elegant dining room of the main house, is worth getting out of bed for. *$$–$$$; AE, MC, V; checks OK; www.starrettmansion.com.*

Ashland Springs Hotel

212 E Main St, Ashland, OR; 541/488-1700 or 888/795-4545

Old Hollywood glamour abounds at this historic hotel. Built in 1925, it was once considered the most luxurious hotel between San Francisco and Portland. Today, the boutique hotel's old-style architecture—ornate chandeliers and tiny rooms with the tall, original 1920s windows—is enhanced with a pretty naturalist theme. A shell, bird, and floral motif decorates guest rooms and the comfortable lobby, where weary travelers can settle into cozy sofas and watch Ashland's bustling Main Street through the windows. More private places to relax are the elegant mezzanine and the shaded outdoor patio located off the hotel's second floor. Guests can also dine at the hotel's adjacent restaurant, Lark, which offers farm-to-table comfort cuisine in an inviting setting. *$$–$$$; AE, DIS, MC, V: checks OK; www.ashlandspringshotel.com.*

Autumn Leaves Bed and Breakfast

2301 21st St, Anacortes, WA; 360/293-4920

Most folks pass through Anacortes only briefly on their way to the San Juan Islands, but this bed-and-breakfast just may give romantic travelers a reason to stop and discover the unknown charms. Decorated throughout with exquisite antiques, Autumn Leaves combines elegant Victorian touches with modern amenities. Each of the three rooms boasts a two-person jetted tub, and gas fireplaces create a distinctive atmosphere with all the creature comforts desired in a romantic getaway. With views of Mount Baker in the distance, the King Louis Room, accented in rich ruby tones, is our favorite. The delicious breakfast, served in the dining room, is a highlight, featuring delightful dishes like French toast, lemon crepes, and frittatas. *$$$; MC, V; checks OK; www.autumn-leaves.com.*

Beaconsfield Inn

998 Humboldt St, Victoria, B.C.; 250/384-4044 or 888/884-4044

Owners Bob and Dawna Bailey uphold the tradition of Old World elegance that has long been the hallmark of this beautifully restored Edwardian manor, located just a few blocks from the downtown core. As you pass through a plant-filled sun-room with fountain to the main entrance, with its rich mahogany walls and roaring fireplace, you'll feel immediately at home. A full afternoon tea, with pastries, crumpets, and scones, or evening sherry is served in the impressive library, where walls of bookcases and a fireplace provide a cozy ambience. Fresh flowers from the garden await in each of the nine guest rooms. Choosing from among so many delightful options can be difficult, but rest assured, all the rooms have gorgeous antiques, fine linens, down comforters, and lovely color schemes. The friendly hosts and staff are professional, unobtrusive, and readily available, and a complimentary full breakfast is served at intimate dining room tables or by the fountain in the adjacent conservatory. *$$$–$$$$; AE, MC, V; no checks; www.beaconsfieldinn.com.*

Betty Macdonald Farm

11835 99th Ave SW, Vashon Island, WA; 206/567-4227 or 888/328-6753

This B&B is tucked among 6 acres of 350-year-old trees and has sweeping views of Puget Sound and Mount Rainier, so it's not difficult to imagine that its namesake and former resident found the spectacular setting an inspiring spot to write many of her books, including the children's beloved Mrs. Piggle-Wiggle series. The furnishings are aged and amenities a bit dated, so if you are looking for true elegance you might search elsewhere, though lodging options on Vashon are limited. What you will certainly find are wonderful views and lush gardens full of Asian pear trees, raspberries, and walnuts. Nearby trails lead through lush wooded areas to the beach below, and you will pass several splendid sitting areas along the way. The spacious All Cedar Loft provides the best view, which can be enjoyed from the room's private deck. The Cottage has a six-foot-long, claw-foot tub flanked by windows on all sides, through which you can peer into the orchids and across the vast Puget Sound to Mount Rainier. Both accommodations are rustic and filled with mixture of Oriental rugs, eclectic antiques, and books galore. They also both have self-catering kitchens and are stocked with makings for a continental breakfast. *$$–$$$; no credit cards; checks OK; www.bettymacdonaldfarm.com.*

Blue Fjord Cabins

862 Elliott Rd, Lopez Island, WA; 360/468-2749 or 888/633-0401

Sequestered beneath groves of cedar and fir trees, these cabins provide a total escape from everything but each other. Both chalet-style cabins are simply decorated and feature skylights and open-beam ceilings. The Norway cabin, hidden among the cedars, is best for couples who enjoy long, leisurely mornings. The Sweden Cabin catches the morning light—perfect for early risers looking to explore. Each cabin has a voluptuous queen-size bed with featherbed and duvet, a fully equipped kitchen, a TV, a secluded deck with forest views, and utter privacy. Seashells mark the beginning of a five-minute nature-trail walk to a "minifjord" in Jasper Bay. Savor the stillness as you snuggle in the private gazebo on the beach, by far the best place to kiss, with its stunning view of Mount Baker. Catch a glimpse of your only other neighbors: bald eagles, blue herons, and sea otters. Since this isn't a bed-and-breakfast, stock up in Lopez Village before arriving. *$$; no credit cards; checks OK; www.bluefjord.com.*

Bonneville Hot Springs Resort & Spa

1252 E Cascade Dr, North Bonneville, WA; 866/459-1678

For a restorative splurge, escape to Washington's premier hot-springs resort and spa. One look at the three-story lobby, with its river-rock fireplace and floor-to-ceiling windows, and you'll know you're in for a treat. Inside, enjoy one of 78 guest rooms, many with hot tubs containing the resort's healing mineral spring water. Outside, explore the beautifully landscaped grounds, with pools, hot tubs, saunas, hiking trails, and putt-putt golf. The real highlight, however, is the range of more than 40 inspiring spa treatments, from mineral baths and body wraps to facials, massages, and reflexology. On-site wine tasting is available on weekends, and the resort's restaurant, Pacific Crest Dining Room (509/427-9711), serves healthful Northwest cuisine. *$$$$; AE, DIS, MC, V; checks OK; www.bonnevilleresort.com.*

Boreas Bed & Breakfast Inn

607 N Ocean Beach Blvd, Long Beach, WA; 360/642-8069 or 888/642-8069

Just as Boreas, the god of the north wind, brought clear weather to the Greeks, this bed-and-breakfast bearing his name will make clouds of stress disappear for amorous couples. The home is tightly tucked between other houses, but this will be forgiven once you see the spectacular coastal setting and the lovely interior—including a marble fireplace and baby grand piano in the living room. Choose from five gracious guest rooms, three of which have ocean views. The delicious breakfast served family-style at the dining room table might include omelets filled with wild mushrooms and smoked salmon, ginger pancakes with lime sauce, or French toast topped with Grand Marnier and almonds, along with organic coffee, hot chocolate, or one of dozens of teas. Don't forget to sign up for your time in the state-of-the art spa located in an enclosed cedar and glass gazebo in the dunes—it's reserved for one couple at a time, so you can cherish your sunset soak in supreme privacy, with the gentle rustle of beach grass as a heavenly soundtrack. *$$$; AE, DC, MC, V; checks OK; www.boreasinn.com.*

Brentwood Bay Lodge & Spa

849 Verdier Ave, Victoria, B.C.; 250/544-2079 or 888/544-2079

This modern cedar-sided resort provides a relaxing, pleasure-filled getaway among the Saanich Peninsula's wineries, organic farms, and sheltered coves, 20 minutes from downtown Victoria. Windows and private balconies in all 33 rooms overlook the marina and forested hills; for more privacy and less noise, request rooms away from the restaurant and pool. The decor is hip West Coast: serene sage-green colors, gas fireplaces, handcrafted king-size beds, sunset tubs or jetted showers, and an outdoor pool and hot tub overlooking the bay. Splurge in the resort's spa with the decadent couples room for massages, mud wraps, and a private rain-forest shower for two. Bask in this serene vibe or enjoy the opportunity to take an eco-cruiser, a water taxi, or a kayak paddle to nearby Butchart Gardens. Enjoy your sparkling local wine greeting, and keep things cozy by opting for breakfast in bed. The Brentwood Seagrille and Pub beckons couples with its stellar views and stand-out cuisine. *$$$$; AE, MC, V; no checks; www.brentwoodbaylodge.com.*

Brookside Inn

8243 NE Abbey Rd, Carlton, OR; 503/852-4433

Thoreau might have traveled to this tranquil lakeside retreat to enjoy a quiet weekend in the woods. The surrounding property is the main draw with its private pond, burbling streams, and dozens of romantic wooded trails. The pond's tiny island is perfectly sized for a two-person picnic or an evening stargazing session. Afterward, retreat to the cozy outdoor fire pit or one of nine simple guest rooms. Of them, we recommend the Kittiwake room with its four-poster bed and silky winter-white linens, though its stark bathroom isn't exactly romance inspiring. The smaller, adjacent Mackintosh room comes furnished with a lovely claw-foot tub and lodge-style furnishings. In the morning, nibble warm scones, fruit, yogurt, and homemade granola before the main country-style breakfast is served in the dining room overlooking a picturesque stream. *$$$–$$$$; AE, DC, MC, V; checks OK; www.brooksideinn-oregon.com.*

Channel House

Ellingson St, Depoe Bay, OR; 541/765-2140 or 800/447-2140

Perched high on the cliffs of Depoe Bay, this towering-yet-unexceptional building reveals little about the magic found inside. The interior of this cozy getaway features a nautical theme, from the whales etched into the glass entrance doors to guest rooms with names like Channel Watch, the Bridge, and Crow's Nest. Most of the 17 units are suites and nearly all feature views of waves crashing against the coastline. The larger, more desirable oceanfront rooms and suites have their own private decks, where you can lie back in a steaming hot tub for two and watch the evening sun disappear into the sea. Most popular and romantic is the Admiral Suite, a top-floor corner affording spectacular views that make you feel at times that you're actually at sea. The suite features a queen-size bed, gas fireplace, and whirlpool on the deck. Each room comes equipped with a pair of binoculars for whale watching, and several units offer the additional convenience of full kitchens and small kitchenettes. In the morning, head downstairs to the ocean-view dining room for a buffet of fresh fruit and pastries. *$$$–$$$$; AE, DIS, MC, V; checks OK; www.channelhouse.com.*

A Cowslip's Belle Bed & Breakfast

159 N Main St, Ashland, OR; 541/488-2901 or 800/888-6819

Each of the five rooms at this retreat (two in the 1913 bungalow and three in the adjacent carriage house) is named for a flower mentioned in a Shakespeare play. Our favorite rooms are the carriage house accommodations, each with a private entrance, a down comforter, and the softest linens you've ever snuggled in. Air-conditioning in all rooms provides comfort during the sweltering heat of Ashland's summers. The morning meal at Cowslip's Belle is an event in itself. (The innkeepers also operate a popular cookie company, so you know the treats have got to be good!) Served on the main floor of the bungalow, breakfast may include fresh fruit, homemade coffee cake, and sour cream Belgian waffles with pecan maple syrup or cornmeal crepes with shrimp-vegetable stuffing. *$–$$$; MC, V; checks OK; closed Nov–Feb; www.cowslip.com.*

Cozy Rose Inn Bed and Breakfast

1220 Forsell Rd, Grandview, WA; 800/575-8381

This cozy country retreat nestled into a landscape of orchards, ponds, waterfalls, and vineyards offers a romantic stop for wine tasters and passersby. Five suites housed in separate structures with private entrances range from cozy to plush. Each has a fireplace, a large jetted tub and shower, a satellite TV, wi-fi, and fresh flowers. We recommend the two suites on the upper floor. Suite Surrender, decorated in Italian style, boasts views of Mount Rainier and oceans of vineyards. A large Jacuzzi tub and shower big enough for four is sure to start some good, clean fun. Guests in the Villa Vista Suite enjoy French-influenced decor, a canopy bed, and a rooftop deck. Breakfast is delivered to each room. Dinner is also available upon request and is based on inn occupancy. The trail to the family vineyard calls for a romantic stroll for two. Don't overlook the llamas: they like to give kisses too. *$$–$$$; MC, V; checks OK; www. cozyroseinn.com.*

The DreamGiver's Inn

7150 NE Earlwood Rd, Newberg, OR; 503/476-2211

Come for a breath of fresh air at this four-bedroom country-style inn. The inviting red house beckons with its wide porch, surrounding viewing gardens, manicured lawns, and acres of land for wooded wandering. Once inside, guests will also enjoy a cozy fireside lounge located next to each of four guest rooms. Of them, we found the Faith suite—often reserved by honeymooners—particularly lovely. Decorated in a warm yellow and black motif, this room boasts a four-poster bed, an in-suite bathroom, and an oversize window chair that overlooks valley views. The quaint Courage suite also charmed us with its gold and mauve hues, antique bed, and luxurious linens. Breakfasts here are a decadent family-style affair and might feature sweet crème brûlée French toast, fresh fruit, yogurt, granola, sausage, coffee cake, and homemade muffins—all in one sitting. Afterward, retreat to your room and cuddle on your spacious window seat with a good book—or simply with each other. *$$$; AE, DIS, MC, V; checks OK; www.dreamgiversinn.com.*

Eagle Rock Lodge

49198 McKenzie Hwy, Vida, OR; 541/822-3630 or 888/773-4333

It's a trek to get to this riverside lodge located along the McKenzie River some 40 miles from Eugene, but it's worth it. The eight rooms each present unique appeal, whether it's with a Jacuzzi tub for two, a handsome fireplace and sitting area, or a river view. Wake up to views of the lush McKenzie River from the three-room Riverview Suite, which has multiple sitting areas, a carved four-poster queen-size bed, and a cozy woodstove. Or, seek even more spacious lodging in the Fireplace Suite situated just off the backyard deck. This large suite has a cabin feel with a queen-size bed, rustic decor, and a stately fireplace. Feast on elegantly presented three-course breakfasts that might include fruit, a homemade cinnamon-roll ring, and a main course of house-made sausage patties, vegetable frittata, roasted potatoes, and fresh tomatoes. Note that nearby eateries don't compare to the cuisine served here—or anywhere in Eugene. Each room comes equipped with a microwave and mini fridge, and owners Randy and Debbie Dersham keep the common room stocked with chocolates, cookies, and wine. *$$–$$$; MC, V; checks OK; www.eaglerocklodging.com.*

English Bay Inn

1968 Comox St, Vancouver, B.C.; 604/683-8002 or 866/683-8002

Chances are good that once you settle in, you won't want to leave this English Tudor hotel located in the heart of Vancouver's West End. What really sets this inn apart from the others is its prime location, a mere block away from Stanley Park. Appealing touches include complimentary sherry and port, sumptuous Ralph Lauren linens, and a full breakfast that typically features eggs and homemade scones. The best suite is room 5, a bilevel hideaway with a fireplace, jetted tub, and loft bedroom with skylight. *$$$–$$$$; AE, DC, DIS, MC, V; no checks; www.englishbayinn.com.*

FivePine Lodge

1021 Desperado Trail, Sisters, OR; 541/549-5200 or 866/974-5900

At this luxurious retreat, the sustainably built cabins, lodge, and conference center sit surrounded by pine trees and a meandering stream. Owners Zoe and Bill Willitts have spent 12 years envisioning and building a space for couples to reconnect. All rooms feature private patios or decks, stone fireplaces, and delicious king-size beds. Each of the five Romance Cabin suites also boasts a soaking tub with a natural water feature and a large double-headed walk-in shower. Access to the Sisters Athletic Club, a healthy breakfast, an evening wine reception, and use of the center's cruiser bikes are all included with your stay. Be sure to book the best amenity of all: a spa service at the Shibui Spa. The Sisters' Movie House and the seasonally focused Pleiades restaurant are also located on-site. *$$$; AE, DIS, MC, V; checks OK; www.fivepinelodge.com.*

Freestone Inn

31 Early Winters Drive, Mazama, WA; 509/996-3906 or 800/639-3809

This Northwest lodge, in the fullest and most gracious use of the word, is lovely: comfortable with rugged refinement. A two-story log structure overlooking Freestone Lake offers guests trout fishing in summer and ice skating in winter. An enormous stone fireplace in the Great Room divides the sitting room from the dining room. Remote and romantic, this is a blend of rustic country with warm, welcoming furnishings. All guest rooms and suites have lake views and feature king-size beds, wrought-iron or pine furniture, cozy gas fireplaces, and private patios or decks. The Early Winter Cabins are set on Early Winters Creek adjacent to the lodge and are extremely private. Cabin sizes vary from studio to two bedrooms, and the decor has a simpler country feel. Jack's Hut (509/996-2752) across the parking lot can arrange everything from horseback riding and fly-fishing to mountain biking, hiking, and whitewater rafting. *$$$; AE, MC, V; checks OK; www.freestoneinn.com.*

Greenlake Guesthouse

7630 E Greenlake Dr N, Seattle, WA; 206/729-8700 or 866/355-8700

Situated beside one of Seattle's most popular destinations, the four tastefully appointed guest rooms in this 1920 Craftsman differ slightly in character and amenities. Cozily romantic without being fussy, Parkview, our favorite, has a picture window facing the lake. The largest of the rooms, it features a sitting area with a daybed and jetted tub for two with separate shower. Though it can be hard to leave your oh-so-comfortable bed in the morning, the full gourmet breakfast (including freshly baked pastries and favorites like Swedish pancakes and omelets) served in the communal dining room isn't to be missed—nor is a Green Lake stroll: it's one of the must-do Seattle pastimes. *$$–$$$; DIS, MC, V; no checks; www.green lakeguesthouse.com.*

Guest House Log Cottages

24371 SR 525, Greenbank, WA; 360/678-3115

Surrounded by acres of meadows and forest, the Guest House Log Cottages are set in a pastoral wonderland, perfect for those seeking woodsy seclusion robust with rustic charms. Five quaint cottages and one spectacular lodge are spread out across the property, affording the level of privacy hoped for in a romantic retreat. Inside, the cabins all feature old-fashioned country touches like patchwork quilts and rustic oak furniture, while also offering several appealing amenities, including Jacuzzi tubs, fireplaces, and kitchens. Serious romantics should consider splurging on the larger and more luxurious lodge. With soaring cathedral ceilings and floor-to-ceiling windows overlooking the grounds, the grand log house sets the stage as an exquisite backdrop for a special occasion. A heated swimming pool (open seasonally) and an outdoor hot tub are also available for guests to enjoy. *$$$–$$$$; DIS, MC, V; checks OK; www.guest houselogcottages.com.*

Halfmoon Bay Cabin

8617 Redrooffs Rd, Halfmoon Bay, B.C.; 604/885-0764 or 866/333-2468

Set on a forested hill overlooking the water, this private log cabin is an ideal retreat for couples seeking a weekend of luxurious seclusion. Large and well appointed, the cabin is spacious enough for four people to stay comfortably, but is a delightful splurge for two. On the sprawling sundeck, enjoy the rare delight of an outdoor shower, or grill up a dinner on the barbecue before turning in to nuzzle in front of the living room's wood-burning fireplace. With a beachside cabana at the bottom of the hill, you'll likely want to spend your days sunning and swimming along the cabin's quiet stretch of waterfront. For a truly unforgettable evening, hire local chef Alan Barnes to prepare a gourmet feast beachside. *$$$; MC, V; no checks; www.halfmoonbaycabin.com.*

Harrison House Bed & Breakfast

2310 NW Harrison Blvd, Corvallis, OR; 541/752-6248 or 800/233-6248

Set in a quaint neighborhood just blocks from downtown, Harrison House boasts a country ambience and a close-in location perfect for exploring the Corvallis's restaurants and public parks. Here each of four rooms (all with private baths) provide vintage charm, but we recommend the private backyard Cottage Suite with its queen-size bed, full bath, kitchenette, and French doors that open to a semiprivate patio overlooking a peaceful garden. This historic Dutch Colonial–style bed-and-breakfast has flourished under the direction of new owners Hilarie Phelps and Allen Goodman, who stock the sunroom with complimentary local wines for afternoon sipping and provide truffles in guest rooms upon arrival. These one-time restaurateurs have also garnered a reputation for their exquisite breakfast spreads that feature fresh, seasonal fruit from the Corvallis farmers market and—if you are lucky in love—Goodman's marvelous hazelnut-crusted French toast. *$$; AE, DIS, MC, V; checks OK; www.corvallis-lodging.com.*

Harrison House Suites

235 C St, Friday Harbor, WA; 360/378-3587 or 800/407-7933
The five suites in this sweet bed-and-breakfast each have their own distinct character, while featuring the same amenities: gas fireplaces, private decks, hot tubs, and fully stocked kitchens. The Orcas Suite, affectionately nicknamed the "honeymoon suite," has water, sunrise, and sunset views. The Roche Harbor Cottage, a separate building with a private entrance, has a full kitchen and private hot tub. Its front deck overlooks the wildflower garden. Complimentary bicycles are ready for a romantic ride and kayaks are set to sail for a sunset cruise. A four-course gourmet breakfast is served in the Garden Café or delivered at a prearranged time. *$$$$; MC, V; checks OK; www.harrisonhousesuites.com.*

Hartmann House

5262 Sooke Rd, Sooke, B.C.; 250/642-3761
With lit paths leading you through a resplendent English cottage garden, this handcrafted, cedar-sided home sets the stage for your own private romance beginning with separate garden entrances to two large, self-contained suites full of enjoyable treats: a whirlpool tub for two, a handmade wooden shower stall, a double-sided fireplace, a kitchenette, a TV and stereo, wide-plank fir floors, and fluffy robes. Expect warm welcomes with fruit, cheese, champagne, and chocolates, and then enter into quiet seclusion. The slightly larger Honeymoon Suite was built around a four-poster "barley-twist" king-size canopied bed, hand-carved from western red cedar. (It's one of the most romantic beds we've ever seen!) Carefully selected decor and gorgeous woodwork lend elegance to this open, light-filled room. The Hydrangea Suite is similarly luxurious, with a sleigh bed and French doors leading to a secluded garden patio. In the morning, a decadent breakfast is subtly delivered to your room. *$$$; MC, V; no checks; www.hartmannhouse.bc.ca.*

The Honey Moon Cabin on Marrowstone Island

1460 East Marrowstone Rd, Nordland, WA; 509/662-0849 or 509/630-2119

Secluded in 6 acres of woods and connected to the mainland by a small bridge, this cabin, located 20 minutes from Port Townsend, is a spectacular romantic destination. The woods are filled with paths to explore, and a short walk reveals a rocky beach with remarkable views of the Olympics and Puget Sound. The cabin itself is essentially one large room, filled with lovely furnishings and cozy comfort. Almost as big as the main room, the bathroom has a glass-block shower and giant Jacuzzi tub. Outside, the wraparound deck is perfect for barbecuing and enjoying the surrounding tranquility. The cabin features a kitchen stocked with all the breakfast fixings you'll need, plus extra goodies like a complimentary bottle of wine, champagne, and chocolates. *$$$; no credit cards; checks OK; www. olympicgetaway.com.*

Husum Highlands Bed & Breakfast

70 Postgren Rd, Husum, WA; 509/493-4503 or 800/808-9812

When you're 7 miles off Highway 14 and winding way up a gravel road, it's easy to wonder if you took a wrong turn—until you pull up to this beautiful, well-maintained home framed by what's easily the most stunning view of Mount Hood. The view alone makes a stay in this five-room bed-and-breakfast worthwhile, and—with hot tub, gazebo, and lingering spaces—there is plenty of opportunity and privacy to soak it up. Melanie's Suite offers the most privacy and best views both of Mount Hood and the manmade waterfall. In addition to preparing delicious breakfasts, owners Carol and Jerry Stockwell will also provide shuttle services for bike rides and picnic excursions, arrange in-house massages, and share great areas to recreate. Or, you can just stay put and blissfully snuggle up and enjoy the beauty right in front of you. *$$–$$$; MC, V; checks OK; www.husumhighlands.com.*

Inn on Orcas Island

114 Channel Rd, Deer Harbor, WA; 360/376-5227 or 888/886-1661

This spectacular luxury inn is set on 6 acres overlooking an estuary at the top of Deer Harbor. The building is reminiscent of a weather-aged Cape Cod and fits in beautifully with the surroundings. Owners John Gibbs and Jeremy Trumble, who were formerly in the art business, have lined the walls with artwork; well-chosen colors and beautiful furnishings fill the eight rooms in the main house, the carriage house, and the stunning cottage. Expect luxurious amenities such as 300-thread-count sheets and heated floors; rooms also have phones and data ports (some have TVs). The two beautifully decorated king suites feature slate-tiled fireplaces and jetted tubs in the spacious bathrooms. Breakfast includes treats like coffee cake, fresh orange yogurt, and eggs Florentine. Bikes are available to guests, and kayaking and whale trips that leave from Deer Harbor are just a few steps away. For all lovers, this is an idyllic spot. *$$$–$$$$; AE, MC, V; checks OK; www.theinnonorcasisland.com.*

The James House

1238 Washington St, Port Townsend, WA; 360/385-1238 or 800/385-1238

This striking Queen Anne home is as Victorian as it gets in Port Townsend. And, since it's set right on the bluff overlooking town and Puget Sound, the view is totally unobstructed. Most of the 12 guest rooms have impressive water views, and all have private baths. The elegant Bridal Suite, with its unsurpassed water and mountain views, soft lighting, wood-burning fireplace, and complimentary champagne, is the most grand. Freshly baked cookies in the afternoon and complimentary sherry are nice extras, but the real treat is the full breakfast, which may include fresh scones, baked pear with walnut-fruit filling, and a tasty egg dish. Next door, a modest, more contemporary brick house holds another romantic lodging called A Bungalow on the Bluff, managed by the James House. To be perfectly honest, kissing here is inevitable. *$$; AE, DIS, MC, V; checks OK; www.jameshouse.com.*

Lara House Lodge

640 NW Congress St, Bend, OR; 541/388-4064 or 800/766-4064

This beautifully remodeled 1910 Craftsman on a quiet residential corner near downtown Bend features a light-filled sunroom, garden deck, and large front porch framing views of tranquil Drake Park and Mirror Pond. All six guest rooms are luxurious, with sumptuous king- or queen-size beds and private baths, some with old-fashioned tubs, some with Jacuzzis. For the utmost in intimacy, we favor the third-floor Summit Suite, tucked under the eaves with a king-size bed, a cozy living room, and original artwork. A nightly turndown service with chocolates and spa-quality bath products will remind you that you are somewhere special. In the afternoon, enjoy delicious food and wine selections in the Great Room. In the morning, feast on a generous gourmet breakfast featuring house-made pastries, seasonal fruit, crepes, quiches, or chili-cheese puffs; genuine smiles from the innkeepers are always present. *$$$–$$$$; AE, DC, DIS, MC, V; www.larahouse.com.*

Lighthouse Bed and Breakfast

650 Jetty Rd SW, Bandon, OR; 541/347-9316

If you do nothing else here but cuddle up and take in the stunning views, your stay will be memorable. This spacious, warm contemporary house is oriented toward the mouth of the Coquille River, which means guests get front-row seats for the lighthouse, the river, and the ocean. At any given moment you might spy windsurfers, seals, or seabirds—or maybe even a migrating whale. All five rooms are spacious, with private baths and homey decor. Our favorite is the Gray Whale Room with a California king bed and whirlpool tub for two overlooking the spectacular view of the Pacific Ocean, river, and Bandon Lighthouse. Breakfast specialties include three-cheese quiche, fruit platters, croissants, homemade muffins, and French toast. *$$; MC, V; checks OK; www.lighthouselodging.com.*

Lion and the Rose Victorian Bed & Breakfast

1810 NE 15th Ave, Portland, OR; 503/287-9245 or 800/955-1647

This historically designated 1906 Queen Anne mansion, located one block from busy NE Broadway, offers excellent access to shopping and dining in Portland's Irvington neighborhood. Each of the seven guest rooms meets a high standard of Victorian elegance, and the hosts let few details go untended, with candles, in-room beverages, and luxurious robes. The spacious Lavonna Room, boasting a marble shower and private bath, wins our hearts. Light, airy lavender and green decor immediately beckons, and the tower window reading nook is perfect for two (with or without a book of Shakespeare's sonnets). Joseph's Room, with its rich red and gold tones, fainting sofa, and lavish four-poster bed, distinctively sets the stage for romance. For its beautiful garden view and the home's only Jacuzzi tub, the first-floor Rose Room is another sweet retreat. Guests are greeted with afternoon tea, and the hearty morning meal is served around a large formal table. *$$–$$$; AE, DIS, MC, V; checks OK; www.lionrose.com.*

Lonesome Cove Resort

416 Lonesome Cove Rd, Friday Harbor, WA; 360/378-4477

Drive down the long, wooded gravel road and into the dreamy, sepia-colored past to secluded Lonesome Cove Resort, located on the northernmost part of the island. Six cabins with vintage Lincoln Log charm skirt a private pebbled beach, their decks and living rooms looking out across the channel to Spieden Island. On a hill above the cabins you can sit (and kiss!) in solitude on a wooden bench beside a trout-stocked pond. Inside the cozy cabins, huge stone fireplaces, exposed log walls, and full kitchens will help you relax in unfussy comfort. For those arriving by water, a 100-foot private dock with power and water is available May through

October. Be sure and stock up in Friday Harbor or Roche Harbor. Once you've settled in, you won't want to leave. *$$; MC, V; checks OK; www. lonesomecove.com.*

Lost Mountain Lodge

303 Sunny View Dr, Sequim, WA; 360/683-2431 or 888/683-2431

This soothing lodge on 6 acres of sunny meadows is the very definition of easygoing romance. Its unfussy decor, vaulted ceilings, and airy spaces are delightfully refreshing and immediately calming; stepping into its spaces creates an *aah* feeling. Built for romance, every suite has a wood-burning fireplace and king-size bed, as well as a private bathroom stocked with tea lights, lavender bath salts, and French toiletries. (Our favorite is the new Hideaway on Quail Lake, the largest, most luxurious, and most private suite.) The owners are gracious hosts who delight in providing thoughtful treats throughout your stay, including resort-quality robe and slippers and decadent crab dip and cider delivered to your room shortly after your arrival. *$$$–$$$$; MC, V; checks OK; www. lostmountainlodge.com.*

Miller Tree Inn

654 E Division St, Forks, WA; 360/374-6806

Romantic accommodations are hard to come by in this area, but this pretty white house located in Forks offers comfortable options—and, as a bonus, allows kids and pets. The two deluxe suites at the back of the house are the most romantic rooms by far. Very private and quiet, each of these contemporary suites offers views of the surrounding farmlands, a king-size bed, a gas fireplace, a Jacuzzi tub for two, a TV/VCR, and a love seat. An abundant breakfast is served in the morning; the gingerbread pancakes are amazing. With the Hoh Rain Forest 45 minutes away and the Olympic beaches only 20, this is a snug retreat from which to explore this rugged region. *$$–$$$; DIS, MC, V; checks OK; www.millertreeinn.com.*

Morgan Hill Retreat

1921 NE Sawdust Hill Rd, Poulsbo, WA; 360/598-4930 or 800/598-3926

Located only about an hour's traveling time from downtown Seattle, this magical B&B feels worlds away. Proprietress Marcia Breece offers three rooms, two with private entrances. Upstairs, the aerielike Hideaway is a complete apartment, featuring a living room, kitchen, bedroom, and lovely bath. The ground-level Sunflower Suite offers a luxurious king bed and large jetted tub and spacious shower. (In-room massages can be scheduled.) Mountain views are spectacular and the grounds feature a labyrinth and the summertime aroma of 200 lavender plants. (However,

Breece uses fragrance-free organic cleansers and detergents throughout the property's interior.) Fauna is integral to the Morgan Hill experience: in addition to llamas, geese, ducks, chickens, sheep, and Howard the bichon frisé, look for wading birds noshing at the trout pond. It's delightful to relax on the wraparound porch on a sunny morning, dining on pecan pancakes and fresh poached eggs. *$$–$$$; MC, V; no checks; www.morganhillretreat.com.*

Mt. Ashland Inn

550 Mt Ashland Rd, Ashland, OR; 541/482-8707 or 800/830-8707
Sheltered by pine trees near the summit of Mount Ashland, this hand-crafted cedar inn provides an extraordinarily romantic Northwest alpine-lodge experience. Arrive early enough to take a stroll through the woods, then take a dip in the outdoor hot tub with views of Mounts Shasta and McLoughlin before settling in for a gloriously private night in one of five serene guest rooms. Days here begin with a full breakfast that may include chilled mango and kiwi soup or spiced cran-apple pears, followed by an entrée such as toasted almond–cheese French toast. Amenities also include a Finnish cedar sauna and large outdoor spa. Consider bringing a takeout supper from town, as there are no dinner dining options near the inn — plus, once you check in, you'll never want to leave. *$$$; DIS, MC, V; no checks; www.mtashlandinn.com.*

Mt. Hood Hamlet Bed and Breakfast

6741 Hwy 35, Mount Hood, OR; 541/352-3547 or 800/407-0570
A better setting for this New England–style Colonial would have been hard to find. Not only does it overlook the 9-acre farm where owner Paul Romans was raised, but magnificent Mount Hood appears close enough to touch. Paul and his wife, Diane, make it their mission to ensure that the two of you are spoiled every step of the way. Bask in the outdoor Jacuzzi tub for extraordinary views of Mounts Hood and Adams by day, or for stargazing at night. With the heated deck, you'll stay cozy even when you emerge from the hot, bubbly water. Two of the largest rooms, Vista Ridge and Orchard, both boast Jacuzzi tubs, making them prime kissing quarters. You can see Mount Hood from the soothing water of the tub in Vista Ridge's bathroom; Orchard's fireplace and pair of rocking chairs make it a comfy love nest to behold. The charm and the Colonial theme of the inn are further enhanced by original artwork on the walls and period furnishings. All rooms are equipped with TV/VCRs, and there is a good selection of movies. Plush robes are provided, too. To top all this off, the morning meal here is reason enough to book a stay. Delicious offerings include veggie omelets, smoky sausage, a bottomless basket of freshly baked scones, and *very* local jams and jellies—they're homemade by your hosts. *$$; AE, DIS, MC, V; checks OK; www.mthoodhamlet.com.*

Pine Ridge Inn

1200 SW Century Dr, Bend, OR; 541/389-6137 or 800/600-4095

Set on a bluff above the Deschutes River, this charming luxury inn caters to romantics by offering the ultimate in personal attention and privacy. All 20 guest rooms have well-stocked baths or Jacuzzi tubs and evening turndown service. Suites are spacious with living rooms, gas fireplaces, two-person Jacuzzi tubs, and private porches. For an indulgence, the 900-square-foot Hyde Suite takes the cake: with a luxurious king bedroom, a living/dining room, a two-person Jacuzzi, an adjoining powder room, two decks, and expansive river views, this is the best place to kiss in the inn. In the evening, wine and cheese are served in the communal fireside parlor; in the morning, a delicious complimentary breakfast is set out (including a hot entrée, fruit, and cereals). Inn guests may choose to use the exercise facilities and outdoor pool at the nearby athletic club. Celebrating? Check out the moderately priced romance packages and be greeted with chilled champagne and homemade desserts. *$$$; AE, DC, DIS, MC, V; checks OK; www.pineridgeinn.com.*

Point No Point Resort

10829 W Coast Rd, Sooke, B.C.; 250/646-2020

The pure, rugged beauty of Point No Point, set on a mile of waterfront and 40 acres of untamed wilderness, has offered a sublime retreat from civilization since the 1950s. Today, 24 renovated cabins, all with kitchens, bathrooms, wood-burning fireplaces, and breathtaking water views, cater to those preferring natural beauty over phones and televisions. Sixteen enjoy private deck hot tubs—a truly memorable place to kiss. The Blue Jay and the Otter, two sides of a spacious luxury duplex cabin, have 18-foot-high view windows, marble soaking tubs, and two-person showers. Other romantic choices are the Eagle and the Orca, two standalone log cabins with private outdoor hot tubs and the best views. Trails lead down to an inlet and three gorgeous sandy beaches—yet more fantastic kissing spots. Meals are not included in your stay; however, the dining room serves a highly rated lunch, afternoon tea, and dinner. *$$$; MC, V; checks OK; www.pointnopointresort.com.*

Salisbury House

750 16th Ave E, Seattle, WA; 206/328-8682

This stately 1904 Prairie-style home offers a peaceful retreat on a tree-lined street, even though it's only a block off bustling 15th Avenue. Each of the second-floor guest rooms is a corner room with private bath, sharing a sun porch with a refrigerator. On the lower level is the generous Salisbury Suite, larger than many apartments and the only option with cable television and VCR. It also has a 6-foot whirlpool bath, but if agitation isn't essential, the Lavender Room has a 6-foot-long claw-foot soaking tub. For an extra charge, the Romance Package includes chocolates and a dozen roses. Served in the formal dining room overlooking the lush garden, family-style breakfasts are meatless affairs, but it's hard to miss bacon when there's orange croissant French toast on offer. *$$–$$$; AE, MC, V; checks OK; www.salisburyhouse.com.*

Salish Lodge & Spa

6501 Railroad Ave SE, Snoqualmie, WA; 425/888-2556 or 800/826-6124

More than 1.5 million tourists, locals, and inveterate *Twin Peaks* fans flock to Snoqualmie Falls annually. Most wander through the lodge's common areas, but guest wings are accessible only via key cards, so you can feel free to travel between room and spa in your robe. Be sure to include heated-river-rock massages in a couple's treatment room as part of your stay. If you'd rather be in the great outdoors, adventures abound. When you're ready for meals, the Attic Bistro is cozy and casual, but a candlelit dinner in the Dining Room is a must. Choicest guest rooms overlook the river (none actually face the falls): on a clear night, part the drapes to enjoy the moon glow, open a window to hear the rushing water (most dramatic in early spring with the melting of mountain snows), light a crackling fire, and settle into the two-person pipeless Sanijet bath with built-in mood lighting, flutes of champagne at hand. *$$$–$$$$; AE, DC, DIS, MC, V; checks OK; www.salishlodge.com.*

Salt Spring Vineyards Bed and Breakfast

151 Lee Rd, Salt Spring Island, B.C.; 250/653-9463

Salt Spring Vineyards, created by romantic retreat aficionados Jan and Bill Harkley, combines the luxuries of romance with the seductive setting of a working winery. In the spacious Winery Room, located above the tasting room adjacent to the main house (note that the tasting room opens to visitors at noon), you'll enjoy spectacular views of the terraced vineyard and fir-covered valley from the room and its Juliet balcony. In the colorful bathroom, there's a slipper-shaped soaking tub and a showerhead set directly in the ceiling (no curtains here; the whole room becomes your shower). In the main house, the smaller Vineyard Room has a jetted two-person tub and French doors leading to a large, private outdoor deck. Guests also have access to the outdoor jetted tub, set underneath a flower-covered trellis, which overlooks the vineyard. Both rooms offer tasteful country-style decor, neatly stowed microwaves and fridges, and cozy sitting areas where your breakfast is delivered in the morning; you can enjoy it here or out on your private deck or balcony. *$$; MC, V; checks OK; www.saltspringvineyards.com.*

Sandlake Country Inn

8505 Galloway Rd, Pacific City, OR; 503/965-6745

This secret hideaway boasts no ocean views, but instead offers acres of privacy tucked into gardens of roses, just 1 mile from the ocean. Bountiful flower gardens fill the front yard of this 115-year-old farmhouse, hidden on a quiet country road off the Three Capes Scenic Loop, about 10 minutes north of Haystack Rock. The inn's countrified, farmlike surroundings only hint at the elegance and luxury that await you in the three private suites and creek-side cottage. The spacious four-room Starlight Suite occupies the entire second floor. This romantic hideaway features a half-canopy queen bed and a large private deck overlooking the gardens. A double-sided fireplace warms the master bedroom and extra sitting room, and the suite boasts a luxury bathroom with a double whirlpool tub. In the morning, a decadent four-course breakfast is delivered to your room. *$$; DIS, MC, V; checks OK; www.sandlakecountryinn.com.*

Selah Inn Bed & Breakfast

130 NE Dulalip Landing, Belfair, WA; 360/275-0916 or 877/232-7941

For an entrancing Hood Canal escape, any one of the seven guest suites at Selah Inn fits the bill beautifully. Inside the main house—which also includes a library, a sunroom, a dining room, and an inviting living room with massive stone fireplace—request the King Suite, with its cozy sitting area, large Jacuzzi, fireplace, and luxurious canopied bed looking out to the private deck. The Canal House includes the Beach Suite, one of our favorite waterside escapes on the entire peninsula: it has an incredible view, in addition to a fireplace, deck, and step-up jetted tub—the perfect unwinding spot after clamming or beachcombing. (Incidentally, all guest accommodations feature extra soundproofing for privacy.) Gourmet breakfasts are included, but consider booking dinner, too. You can enjoy elegant multicourse meals featuring fresh local seafood and produce as long as the minimum of four reservations is met. *$$–$$$; MC, V; checks OK; www.selahinn.com.*

Spring Bay Inn

464 Spring Bay Trail, Olga, WA; 360/376-5531

Spring Bay Inn continues to live up to its stellar reputation for romance and relaxation; so much so, we have a difficult time doing it justice. Rain or shine, a guided kayaking adventure along pristine coastline is offered every day. If weather is uncooperative, enjoy a nature walk through the inn's 57 acres and the adjoining Obstruction Pass State Park. So fuel up—Spring Bay offers *two* fresh-made breakfasts—a continental is offered outside your room at 7:30am; after the paddle, a full brunch is served in the common area. The lodge-style inn has a 14-foot-high exposed-beam ceiling, two river-rock fireplaces, and expansive windows overlooking a glorious scene of fir trees, the bay, a small marsh, and a trail leading to the pebbled beach — where a large hot tub awaits. Upstairs, of the four generous guest rooms, the two larger rooms have private decks — excellent for stargazing and the requisite kissing. The main-floor Ranger Suite is the grandest of all with a private entrance, high ceilings, a glass solarium, a wood-burning fireplace, a queen-size bed, and a small private courtyard with soaking tub. *$$$$; DIS, MC, V; checks OK; call for seasonal restrictions; www.springbayinn.com.*

Springbrook Hazelnut Farm Bed & Breakfast

30295 N Hwy 99W, Newberg, OR; 503/538-4606 or 800/793-8528

This vast property, surrounded by lush lawns, gardens, orchards, and a tiny, hidden swimming pool, makes this retreat feel like a secret garden hideaway. Though the rooms in the main house are no longer available, the Carriage House and the Rose Cottage offer some of the most secluded lodging in wine country. Similar in design, each elegant abode has Craftsman-style furnishings, lovely fir floors, large windows, and charming tiled kitchens with glass-front cabinets and big butcher-block tables. They also feature gas fireplaces, queen-size beds, and cream-colored walls with forest-green trim. Popular with honeymooners, the Carriage House offers the most space, but our favorite is the cozy Cottage, with its rose garden, terra cotta–tiled bathroom, and postage-stamp-size dining room overlooking a pond surrounded by irises and daffodils. Breakfast is supplied in the fridge so you needn't rush your morning; delicious treats include cinnamon rolls, ham and asparagus crepes, scones, and fresh fruit. For an incredibly romantic post-breakfast stroll, walk through the hazelnut orchard to the tasting room at Rex Hill Vineyards. Or, visit the historic barn on-site, which houses a one-man operated winery, J. K. Carriere Wines (503/554-0721; www.jkcarriere.com), and another amazing surprise (be sure to ask when you visit). *$$$; MC, V; checks OK; www.nutfarm.com.*

Squalicum Lake Cottage

4367 Squalicum Lake Rd, Bellingham, WA; 360/592-1102

You'll find few settings more serene than what greets you at this contemporary cot-tage, which overlooks a small lake and beautiful gardens that explode with flowers in summer. Once you've come down the rural, tree-lined gravel drive that leads to the property, you may feel as though you're arriving at your own private Walden Pond. The cottage has its own entrance and is separated from the owner's house by landscaping and ornamental grasses. With vaulted ceilings, six skylights, and plenty of windows, the 480-square-foot space is airy and bright. The comfortable main room has a sofa that takes in the view, TV with satellite reception, CD player, and compact but full kitchen. This will come in handy, since the country location means you'll have to drive to enjoy Bellingham's fine dining; it's so peaceful here that the most romantic option may well be to bring provisions and stay in for the evening. The tiny, cozy bedroom has a queen-size bed and basic full bath; you'll find bubble bath and a rubber ducky waiting for your enjoyment. To make the most of your getaway, arrange with the owner for the on-call masseuse to make a house call to the cottage. Other romantic touches include exquisite flower arrange-ments (the owner was formerly a professional florist), Swiss chocolates, and complimentary refresh-ments upon arrival. Breakfast, which is deliv-ered to your door, includes goodies like homemade fruit breads, jams, yogurts, and fresh fruit compotes complete with edible flowers or mint from the owner's organic garden. In warm weather, you can breakfast at the teak table on your own front patio; a day that starts off this beautifully is almost guaranteed to be filled with romance. *$$–$$$ MC, V; checks OK; www.sqlakecottage.com.*

Stephanie Inn

2740 S Pacific St, Cannon Beach, OR; 503/436-2221 or 800/633-3466

The Stephanie Inn exemplifies classic luxury on the edge of the shore. The surf practically laps at the foundations of this New England–style inn, where a fire is always glowing in the river-rock hearth of the front parlor, and overstuffed sofas, impressive wood detailing, and hardwood floors create an inviting and elegant ambience. The inn offers 46 rooms and the adjacent Carriage House contains four more. Rooms are spacious yet cozy with plush terry-cloth robes and four-poster beds made up with beautiful floral linens, and nearly every room has a private deck, gas fireplace, and corner Jacuzzi or whirlpool tub in its spacious bathroom. A complimentary breakfast buffet is served in the inn's mountain-view dining room. During spring and summer the Romantic Beach Bonfire Package includes wood and a starter log and your choice of champagne, wine, or cider. The pack-age also features turndown service with a scattering of rose petals on the bed and a bubble bath awaiting in the Jacuzzi for two. *$$$$; AE, DC, DIS, MC, V; checks OK; www.stephanie-inn.com.*

Tucker House

260 B St, Friday Harbor, WA; 360/378-2783 or 800/965-0123

Friday Harbor is bursting with inns and hotels, but many are on the main drag or just off it—right in the thick of summer tourist craziness. Tucker House, built in 1898, is perched on a hill just two blocks south of the ferry landing—the perfect place from which to join all the craziness or to retreat from it when you're ready for some downtime and a leisurely kiss. The seven rooms and two suites in two houses and the three cottages that comprise Tucker House's property are each named after a quilt-block design and painted in bold or neutral colors to coordinate with the namesake quilt on the bed. All rooms have private baths and TV/VCRs (with a video library in the common area). Breakfast here is simple yet tasty—and delivered to your room at the time you choose (fill out your preference sheet at check-in). A savory, individually baked hot breakfast casserole is accompanied by freshly baked muffins, bagels, granola, yogurt, and fresh fruit; coffee, tea, or hot chocolate and a selection of juices round out the offering. *$$–$$$; MC, V; no checks; www.tuckerhouse.com.*

Turtleback Farm Inn

1981 Crow Valley Rd, Eastsound, WA; 360/376-4914 or 800/376-4914

At dawn, the colors of the countryside come alive. The inn overlooks 80 acres of hills, pastures, ponds, and orchards in the breathtaking Crow Valley. There are rooms in two locations: seven in the beautifully renovated, turn-of-the-century farmhouse, and four in the separate two-story Orchard House. The rooms in the farmhouse, all of which have private baths, range from charming to more charming. The Valley View Room is the most luxurious. Fluffy comforters full of Turtleback Farm's own cozy lamb's wool endow every room with elegant simplicity. Six of the seven baths are outfitted with porcelain and silver antique claw-foot tubs, separate showers, and pedestal sinks—tubs and sinks rescued, after years of romantic service, from the Savoy and Empress hotels. In the separate Orchard House, rooms have similar spacious, elegant bathrooms; taupe walls; polished floors; throw rugs; gas fireplaces; king-size beds; and private decks overlooking the orchard. Although newer, the house doesn't seem to have much soundproofing; we recommend the two top rooms for this reason. The innkeeper, who has published a cookbook, serves a dazzling breakfast, which can be delivered to your room. *$$$; DIS, MC, V; checks OK; www.turtlebackinn.com.*

The Tuwanek Hotel

7545 Islet Pl, Sechelt, B.C.; 604/885-2040 or 800/665-2311

With theme suites for such films as Casablanca and The African Queen, the Tuwanek Hotel is not campy old-Hollywood, as might be expected. Instead, the design is a contemporary twist on old-world glamour, with thematic details—such as hints of animal print in The African Queen suite—subtly employed throughout. The suites, along with the Beach Cottage, blend luxurious amenities, such as a "Cloud Bed"—a Serta Luxury bed with a feather bed on top—outfitted with Egyptian linens, with a charmingly distinctive atmosphere. Downstairs, a game room, snack bar, barbecue, and private movie theater help make this waterfront destination a unique place to put fun back into romance. *$$$; AE, DC, DIS, MC, V; no checks; www.tuwanekhotel.com.*

Villa Marco Polo Inn

1524 Shasta Pl, Victoria, B.C.; 250/370-1524 or 877/601-1524

Villa Marco Polo is a feast for the senses—magnificent rooms, stunning villa-style grounds, and romantic boons like fine linens, flowers, and silver-domed chocolate turndowns. This tastefully restored 1923 Rockland Italian Renaissance–style mansion offers formal beauty and a relaxed adult atmosphere. All five luxurious, soundproof rooms enjoy sublime ambience, but we have three romantic favorites. The second-floor Zanzibar Suite boasts a lovely fireplace, a king bed, a romantically lit bathing haven with double soaking pedestal tub and shower, and French doors to a balcony with mountain, water, and garden views. Equally grand, the Persia Suite offers a lovers' bonus of view seats in a double-jetted tub, Persian rug and tapestries, and a king-size canopy bed. The smaller main-floor Silk Road Room enjoys a barrel vault ceiling and hand-painted angel murals. Roses, champagne, massages, and concierge services are easily arranged here. Mornings bring four-course gourmet breakfasts in the elegant dining room, private garden room, or terrace. *$$$$; MC, V; no checks; www.villamarcopolo.com.*

Woodmark Hotel

1200 Carillon Pt, Kirkland, WA; 425/822-3700 or 800/822-3700

There's plenty of opportunity for intimacy and romance at the Woodmark, particularly if you avoid wedding crowds (it's a very popular knot-tying site), unwind at the serene full-service day spa (remodeled in 2008), and book a room facing the Seattle skyline and Olympic Mountains. All 100 guest-room baths have been upgraded with limestone tile and soaking tub with rain shower (at the minimum), but we like the jetted tubs in the secluded corner Executive Suites. Carillon Point is home to several eateries, including Yarrow Bay Grill. But with a new wine-centric restaurant on the hotel's premises, Cru (425/803-5595), as well as the Library Bar (for proper afternoon tea as well as bar fare), there's little need to step outside. Be sure to ask about a complimentary lake cruise aboard the hotel's 1956 Chris-Craft, and don't miss Raid the Pantry, a complimentary snack buffet laid out in the restaurant nightly at 11:30. *$$$–$$$$; AE, DC, JCB, MC, V; checks OK; www.thewoodmark.com.*

ROMANTIC DINING

Andina Restaurant

1314 NW Glisan St, Portland, OR; 503/228-9535

The inviting terra cotta–toned decor, warm lighting, lively Latin music, and delicious *nueva* Peruvian dishes at this popular Pearl District restaurant are guaranteed to put you into an exotic mood. Start with the tart Peruvian Pisco Sour or the traditional Mexican love potion Granada de Amor—Citroen vodka infused with pomegranate, lime, and Damiana—along with your choice of ceviche and other small plates. Entrées are creative, both in flavor and in presentation, but sure hits include the quinoa-encrusted scallops and the seasonal pork and lamb dishes. House-made desserts—like the quinoa-studded passion-fruit mousse cannoli paired with mango-lemongrass sorbet and caramel—will seduce you with an infusion of Peruvian flavors. *$$$; AE, DIS, MC, V; local checks only; lunch Mon–Sat, dinner every day; full bar; reservations recommended; www. andinarestaurant.com.*

Assaggio Ristorante

2010 4th Ave, Seattle, WA; 206/441-1399

From the moment you set foot in the door you feel the amore, the welcoming tone set by executive chef and owner Mauro Golmarvi. More often than not, he's at the entrance, hailing guests with infectious gusto. High walls are graced by stunning, subtly toned reproductions of works by painters Michelangelo and Fra Lippo Lippi. Tables are positioned close together, and when the restaurant's full—which it usually is—the atmosphere is boisterous, so unless you luck into a booth this may not be the best choice for intimate conversation or a first date. Is the cuisine cutting edge? Nah. This is comfort food, Italian-style. Preparations are simple and simply perfect for sharing, from the *caprese* salad and *insalata di Stefano* (with apples, fennel, pecorino, and truffle oil) to classic fettuccine bolognese and veal piccata. The wine list reaches beyond Tuscany to feature bottles from more obscure Italian regions. *$$–$$$; AE, DC, DIS, MC, V; no checks; lunch Mon–Fri, dinner Mon–Sat; full bar; reservations recommended; www.assaggioseattle.com.*

Baked Alaska

1 12th St, Ste 1, Astoria, OR; 503/325-7414

It's hard to believe that this charming little waterfront restaurant, located at the foot of 12th Street on a dock over the Columbia River, grew out of a mobile soup wagon in Alaska. Back in the '80s, owners Chris and Jennifer Holen coined the phrase "Have soup, will travel" and took their wagon on the road all over the 49th state. The pair retired the wagon and created a romantic little spot in Astoria. Signature dishes include Broiled Pacific Sea Scallops over fresh black pepper linguini tossed with Fuji apples, fennel, and ginger in a light champagne sauce; and Campfire Salmon, prepared in an Alaskan Amber barbecue marinade and flambéed campfire-style. Another favorite is the Thundermuck Tuna, which includes a coffee-dusted albacore tuna seared rare, with a honey-sesame sauce, balsamic reduction, and pickled ginger. To make dining that much sweeter, every seat in the place comes with a view of the Columbia River. *$$; AE, DC, DIS, MC, V; no checks; lunch, dinner every day; full bar; no reservations; www.bakedak.com.*

The Blue Heron Inn

5521 Delta Rd, Sechelt, B.C.; 604/885-3847 or 800/818-8977

Although this old standby desperately needs a floor-to-ceiling remodel, diners still flock here for its unbeatable view of Sechelt Inlet. After almost 20 years as the destination restaurant on the Sunshine Coast, The Blue Heron Inn still serves up tried-and-true favorites. Try one of the fresh seafood dishes available nightly or favorites like the bouillabaisse or the rack of lamb. Although the owner won't accept requests for specific tables, it can't hurt to ask for one by the fireplace in the winter. *$$$$; MC, V; local checks only; dinner Wed–Sun; full bar; reservations recommended.*

Cafe Juanita

9702 NE 120th Pl, Kirkland, WA; 425/823-1505

Sparely decorated in neutral tones, this L-shaped dining room is a serene oasis backed by trees and Juanita Creek, though we prefer the corner table opposite the stone fireplace (by the parking lot), a near-perfect kissing location after dark. For her Northern Italian–inspired menus, chef/owner Holly Smith draws substantially on regional, sustainable, organic products, though the focus sometimes falls on imported treasures, such as Piemontese white truffles. Sweetbreads, foie gras, fresh pastas, and rabbit are outstanding, and every plate is a work of art, from breads and crackers to beautifully arranged desserts. Service is polished and friendly, never intrusive, and we encourage consulting the sommelier about wine: there are 150 Italian reds alone to choose from (though if you're in the mood to splurge, make it a Sassicaia). *$$$; AE, MC, V; local checks only; dinner every day; full bar; reservations recommended; www.cafejuanita.com.*

Café Melange

7 N Front St, Yakima, WA; 509/453-0571

This tiny Italian cafe offers an inviting ambience in the North Front Street Historic District. The cafe has been in the same family for decades, and the delicious Italian recipes all made from scratch and classic red and white decor haven't changed much since the early days. The expanded wine list features more than 100 Washington State wines. Romantically speaking, the modest, plant-adorned interior does not really measure up to the high quality of the meals, although the small linen-draped tables are pleasantly decorated with candles and flowers. It's the superb food here that will arouse your every passion. *$; AE, MC, V; checks OK; lunch, dinner Mon–Sat; beer and wine; reservations recommended; www. cafemelangeyakima.com.*

Canlis Restaurant

2576 Aurora Ave N, Seattle, WA; 206/283-3313

How do we love thee? Let us count the ways. A Seattle institution since 1950, Canlis is recognized as exceptional on all levels, from location and architecture to menu, service, and the world-class 15,000-bottle cellar that has garnered the Wine Spectator Grand Award every year for a decade. Linger over the signature Canlis Salad and Peter Canlis Prawns, Wagyu tenderloin and Muscovy duck breast. Finishing with Grand Marnier soufflé is de rigueur. The kitchen is happy to honor special requests, from nostalgic recipes to vegan tasting menus. Indubitably one of the most romantic nooks in all of Seattle, the Cache is an upstairs corner space for two that comes with a chaise, a telescope, a sound system, its own server, and panoramic views of Lake Union and the Cascades. Naturally, the full-on Canlis experience doesn't come cheap, so if dinner isn't in the cards, soak in the ambience from the lounge over drinks and appetizers while enjoying the live piano music. *$$$$; AE, DC, DIS, MC, V; checks OK; dinner Mon–Sat; full bar; reservations required; www.canlis.com.*

Celilo Restaurant

16 Oak St, Hood River, OR; 541/386-5710

You and your sweetheart will settle right into this contemporary, elegant downtown dining spot with its knowledgeable waitstaff. While Celilo is definitely a popular destination, table placement and acoustics allow for plenty of private conversation. Enjoy food adapted to the agricultural bounty of Hood River and environs with a range of creatively paired meat- and vegetable-based dishes. For starters, try the delicate uovo ravioli appetizer (a single, large stuffed ravioli) and inventive cocktails, and peruse a wine list that highlights many locally produced best-sellers. Desserts, created in-house and perfect for sharing, include both perennial favorites—like the Wy'East Chocolate Volcano Cake and the Apple Tarte Tatin—as well as seasonal options. *$$$; AE, DC, DIS, MC, V; checks OK; lunch, dinner every day; reservations recommended; www.celilo restaurant.com.*

Christina's Restaurant

310 Main St, Eastsound, WA; 360/376-4904

Serving as an island destination for 28 years, this heavenly little spot enjoys a terrific perch above Eastsound and offers fantastic views of the mountains surrounding the inlets. On pretty summer evenings, linger on the open deck at sunset with a glass of wine (from the unique selection). Choose several of the innovative small plates for a cozy shared dinner for two, or each of you can order your own large plate such as the King salmon with lemon cream. Local oysters are routinely on the menu. *$$$; AE, DC, MC, V; checks OK; dinner every day (call for seasonal hours); full bar; reservations recommended; www.christinas.net.*

Cork

150 NW Oregon St, Bend, OR; 541/382-6881

With a cozy, candlelit bar, high-backed booths, and contemporary decor, this restaurant invites its diners to settle in for conversation and "American eclectic" cuisine including lamb shank, prawns and crab, spicy puttanesca, or cioppino. A signature dish is the Black Sesame Pesto-kissed Scallops, which will surely make you swoon. Both the restaurant and wine bar offer an extensive wine list, many served by the glass. To end your meal, you and your sweetheart will relish the French-press coffees and homemade desserts. *$$$; AE, DC, MC, V; no checks; dinner Tues–Sat; beer and wine; reservations recommended; www.corkbend.com.*

Crush

2319 E Madison St, Seattle, WA; 206/302-7874

What better stratagem than to bring a first—or seventh—date to an establishment called Crush? Chef/owner Jason Wilson and his wife, Nicole, gave this 100-plus-year-old Tudor house a crisp, contemporary conversion, and the vibe is youthful and hip. Romantics take note: Crush is crushingly popular, so for a quieter experience we suggest avoiding weekends. Surprisingly comfortable, the restaurant's modern, molded chairs don't exactly facilitate canoodling, but the lighting is flattering, and it's easy to steal a kiss on the warm-weather patio or in the cheek-by-jowl bar. Order an expertly crafted cocktail, particularly anything involving house-infused pear vodka—it'll buy some time to peruse the lengthy global wine list. And then there's the menu, a seasonally rotating, locally and artisanally inspired odyssey that garnered Wilson a Best New Chef Award from *Food & Wine* in 2006. *$$$; AE, DIS, MC, V; no checks; dinner Tues–Sat; full bar; reservations recommended; www.crushonmadison.com.*

Cuvée Restaurant

214 W Main St, Carlton, OR; 503/852-6555

This charming French-influenced restaurant on Carlton's quaint Main Street is simply dressed with black wainscoting, cream walls, white tablecloths, and an artisan chandelier. Dinners here can be quiet, peaceful affairs or a touch crowded depending on the season. Service, however, is always amiable and the cuisine a delight for the senses. French transplant and head chef Gilbert Henry has an esteemed reputation for his pretty presentations and daily fish specials including a breadcrumb-coated salmon served atop silky potatoes beside crisp roasted vegetables. Heartier dishes like a fragrant lamb stew will also please palates. Try the prix-fixe dinner menu featuring an appetizer or dessert, salad, and entrée. *$$$; AE, DIS, MC, V; checks OK; lunch Sat–Sun, dinner Wed–Sun; full bar; reservations recommended; www.cuveedining.com.*

The Depot Restaurant

1208 38th Pl, Seaview, WA; 360/642-7880

This rather ramshackle former train depot might not impress you on first sight (although it looks good for its age, considering the building turned 100 years old in 2005)—but the delicious, creative fare and unique ambience inside will make a lasting impression. For the most romantic atmosphere, reserve a table on the outdoor patio, which is surrounded by ornamental beach grasses and equipped with heat lamps to keep things cozy—you can catch a sea breeze sitting here. The oft-changing menu is satisfyingly American and makes the most of local bounty. You'll find several ways to enjoy local oysters, including a crunchy fried rendition served with garlic aioli. For the main event, try the pan-seared giant prawns and scallops in a ginger-coconut broth with wasabi sticky rice, or one of the constantly changing specials, which are always delicious; steak is always on the menu. Wednesdays bring a fun, build-your-own burger night. Dessert is an absolute must, whether you choose the tiramisù; a seasonal fruit dessert such as a strawberry-rhubarb cobbler; or something decadent, like the chocolate ganache-filled upside-down bread pudding. *$$; DIS, MC, V; checks OK; dinner Tues–Sun (summer), Wed–Sun (winter); beer and wine; reservations recommended; www.depotrestaurantdining.com.*

Dragonfly Bistro & Lounge

633A Front St, Leavenworth, WA; 509/548-7600

For those who like their date nights with a little more spice—both figuratively and literally—this fusion of Japanese, Chinese, Thai, Vietnamese, and American cuisine is an exciting alternative to the many Bavarian choices in town. Innovative menu options include Kobe beef sliders, lavender duck, and Dragonfries—french fries topped with crème fraîche and a drizzle of white truffle oil. Couples who like to get extra close by dancing the evening away will be thrilled—on weekends, the restaurant is set up with a DJ who spins music after 10pm. Sip on sake or a blueberry-ginger Mojito and get your groove on. *$$$; AE, DIS, MC, V; no checks; dinner every day (closed Wed); full bar; reservations recommended; www.dragonfly leavenworth.com.*

Duck Soup Inn

50 Duck Soup Ln, Friday Harbor, WA; 360/378-4878

Duck Soup Inn is the restaurant of choice for island-going lovebirds. Tucked into the woods, the arbor-fronted, shingled cottage overlooks a tranquil pond. The wood-paneled dining room with stone fireplace, wooden booths, and high windows is filled with works by local artists; open-air seating allows for nature's canvas. House specialties comprise the menu, and many of the fresh herbs and edible flowers are grown by chef/owner Gretchen Allison. Apple wood–smoked Westcott Bay oysters appear frequently as starters, and for good reason. Chile rellenos with Jack and goat cheeses and lavender-thyme-crusted free-range chicken breast with blueberry-habanero chutney are favorites for dinner. The wine list is extensive and is easily accessible to nonconnoisseurs, with descriptions such as tropical, fat, buttery, round, polished, sensual, big, spicy, and muscular. So many wines for so many occasions; it's easy to find just the right drink to pair with the evening. *$$; MC, V; no checks; dinner Wed–Sun Apr–Oct (closed Nov–Mar); full bar; reservations recommended; www.ducksoupinn.com.*

El Gaucho

2505 1st Ave, Seattle, WA; 206/728-1337

Look up swank in the dictionary and the name El Gaucho should be there in boldface type. Hearkening back to a bygone era, it's precisely the sort of place befitting Sinatra and his cronies, commanding the room in exquisitely tailored haberdashery. Renowned for exemplary service, a world-class wine program, and tableside preparation of dishes like chateaubriand and bananas Foster, this windowless, bilevel steak house can get a bit loud, but not so much as to compromise your evening— particularly from the sensuous comfort of a mink-lined banquette. All this luxury doesn't come cheap, unless you sup exclusively on sides (modestly priced, except for the criminally rich lobster mashed potatoes). If there's live jazz and dancing in the Pampas Room (90 Wall St; 206/728-1337) downstairs, make a complete night of it, especially if you've procured a room at the boutique inn upstairs. *$$$–$$$$; AE, DC, DIS, MC, V; checks OK; dinner every day; reservations recommended; www. elgaucho.com.*

Fuse Waterfront Grill

5449 Sooke Rd, Sooke, B.C.; 250/642-0011

Recently opened Fuse is a wonderful addition filling a Sooke dining gap. With a beautiful patio and interior space looking out to sailboats at Cooper's Cove, the restaurant combines creative food, a small but good wine list, solid beer offerings, and very reasonable prices. Savor entrées focusing on meats and local seafood with Sooke trout, halibut, and shell-fish green curry, and select from a range of delicious side vegetables including Moroccan yams, braised greens, mashed potatoes, wild rice, or organic salad. As the sun retreats, your waiter will deliver a snuggly blanket and a huge, decadent pot of chocolate fondue for the two of you to share on the patio. *$$–$$$; AE, MC, V; local checks only; lunch, dinner every day (call for winter closures); full bar; reservations recommended; www.fusewaterfrontgrill.com.*

Gogi's Restaurant

235 W Main St, Jacksonville, OR; 541/899-8699

This cozy restaurant tucked off Jacksonville's busy Main Street has flour-ished under new owners; brothers Gabriel and Jonah Murphy entice lov-ers of both romance and fine cuisine. The stylish interior, done in warm colors, rich wood, and cheerful works of art, exudes quiet elegance. The well-stocked bar is the source of tasty mixed drinks and a thorough wine list, which includes selections from local wineries and more worldly vari-etals. Chef Gabriel demonstrates his skills in the kitchen with excellent and eclectic fine-dining fare — crafted with French technique and influenced in Northwest style. For gourmet meals to go, lighter but equally tasty fare is available in Gogi's Britt Boxes. Order these by 2pm to ensure that you'll dine like a gourmand at your Britt Festival show. *$$$; DIS, MC, V; local checks only; brunch Sun, dinner Wed–Sun; full bar; reservations recom-mended; www.gogis.net.*

The Herbfarm Restaurant

14590 NE 145th St, Woodinville, WA; 425/485-5300

Theatrically over-the-top, the resplendent European country house atmo-sphere of this food fanatic's mecca is so fairy-tale fabulous we wouldn't be surprised to see Cinderella pull up in her transformed-gourd carriage. Seasonally themed nine-course tasting menus are always paired with five or six wines from the award-winning cellar (Northwest-focused, 4,000 selections, with a staggering Madeira collection). Unless you specify otherwise, there's a chance you'll be seated at the communal table — entertaining, but not as conducive to romance as a table for two. A clas-sical guitarist performs throughout the five-hour culinary odyssey, and owners Ron Zimmerman and Carrie Van Dyck talk about the evening's offerings between courses. Service is polished and almost psychically attentive: whenever you leave the table a fresh napkin is placed at your seat. Make a special evening transcendent and unforgettable by reserving either the Herb Garden or Orchard House, the Herbfarm's ultraromantic suites at Willows Lodge next door. *$$$$; AE, MC, V; checks OK; dinner Thurs–Sun; full bar; reservations required; www.theherbfarm.com.*

Il Fiasco

2717 6th Ave, Tacoma, WA; 253/272-6688

Whisk away the one you love to enjoy a traditional Italian meal at this delightful restaurant, worthy of any celebration. Called "upscale but down-to-earth" by the *Tacoma News Tribune*, shades of straw and claret provide the wonderful backdrop for the romance of Tuscany. Order one of the pasta specialties, like the Ravioli al Fungi or Linguini alla Cioppino, or one of the decadent entrées, which include such unusual specialties as braised wild boar. For a true splurge, you can't go wrong with an Italian wine off the high-end Captain's List. And, yes, if you're wondering about the name, Il Fiasco is in on the joke, promising that your meal will never be a fiasco. The unusual name instead comes from the straw basket that is wrapped around many bottles of chianti. *$$$; AE, DIS, MC, V; checks OK; lunch Mon–Fri, dinner every day; full bar; reservations recommended; www.ilfiasco.com.*

Macrina Bakery & Cafe

2408 1st Ave (and branches), Seattle, WA; 206/448-4032

Artisanal baker Leslie Mackie has been casting a spell on Seattle for more than a decade, and the enchantment renews each morning as fresh bread, pastry, and the aroma of espresso greet still-sleepy downtown residents and on-the-go commuters. Start your day with homemade bread pudding with fresh fruit and cream, or cinnamon rolls made from Mackie's luscious croissant-style dough. Lunch charms with simple salads, sandwiches, and a meze plate—your choice of three Mediterranean-inspired noshes. Mackie's cookbook (*Leslie Mackie's Macrina Bakery & Cafe Cookbook*) gives a sneak peak into the magic of the café—but don't pass up experiencing the real thing. Locations on Queen Anne (615 W McGraw St; 206/283-5900) and Vashon Island (19603 Vashon Hwy SW; 206/567-4133) offer even more opportunities to indulge. *$; MC, V; local checks only; breakfast, lunch Mon–Fri, brunch Sat–Sun; beer and wine; no reservations; www.macrinabakery.com.*

Marché

296 E 5th Ave, Eugene, OR; 541/342-3612

Lovers with refined palates will appreciate the well-crafted combinations of fresh and often organically grown local foodstuffs at the heart of Marché's meals. This sophisticated restaurant on the ground floor of the Fifth Street Public Market celebrates the seasonal Northwest bounty with menus that change daily and entrées prepared with a French sensibility. In fall, pork chops from local farms may come with an autumn fruit-and-onion confit, and the sage-infused roasted leg of venison is accompanied by sweet-potato purée, baked apple, and huckleberry sauce. Come summer, Oregon albacore is seared rare and served with smoked-tomato *coulis* and fried squash blossom. Lunch is lighter, with the addition of a few *pizzettas* from a wood-fired oven (picture pancetta, delicata squash, sage, and Romano cheese) and sandwiches such as portobello mushroom with sun-dried-tomato relish and smoked mozzarella on homemade flatbread. The wine list and dessert menu reflect the same regional leanings and attention to detail. The interior—elegantly hip with dark, gleaming wood and wry artwork—sets the stage for an enjoyable and tasty evening with your sweetheart. *$$$–$$$$; AE, DC, DIS, MC, V; checks OK; lunch, dinner every day, brunch Sun; full bar; reservations recommended; www.marcherestaurant.com.*

Markus' Wharfside Restaurant

1831 Maple Ave S, Sooke, B.C.; 250/642-3596

This little fisherman's cottage overlooking Sooke Harbour has been transformed into a simple, art-filled Mediterranean restaurant; with just nine tables, the feel is intimate but not crowded. Every table has a water and mountain view, but our favorite space is the fireplace room for its cozy hearth and picture window. European-trained chef Markus Wieland applies his considerable talents to the bounty of wild seafood and organic produce available locally. Starters include Tuscan seafood soup and baked goat cheese with roasted garlic. For a main course, try a local fish or the tempting daily risotto special and enjoy this intimate experience. *$$$; MC, V; no checks; dinner Tues–Sat (call for winter closures); full bar; reservations recommended; www.markuswharfsiderestaurant.com.*

Mona's Bistro and Lounge

6421 Latona Ave NE, Seattle, WA; 206/526-1188

Appealing to a wide age range, Mona's—named for the world's most famous painting—is casually sophisticated yet isn't afraid to let her naughty-girl side show, a high ceiling setting off walls of dusky periwinkle and claret that lend a slightly bordello-ish flavor to the ambience. Fittingly, the bar dominates the room: Mona's mixologists craft beautifully balanced and very grown-up cocktails. Cuisine is Mediterranean Italian, with a rotating menu of dishes too tasty not to share. Music, however, is the romantic icing on the cake: Wednesday through Saturday evenings, Mona's swaps her restaurant mantle for club attire, with alternating nights of a DJ setting the mood with ultralounge beats and live jazz combos that draw a more seasoned crowd. *$$–$$$; AE, DC, DIS, MC, V; no checks; dinner every day, brunch Sun; full bar; reservations recommended; www.monasseattle.com.*

Oliver's Twist

6822 Greenwood Ave N, Seattle, WA; 206/706-6673

Consider yourself . . . at home! With clever food, cleverer cocktails, smooth service, and a comfortably chic environment, this neighborhood haunt is one of our favorites for late afternoon or later evening. The lighting is dim with flickering candles standing in for hissing gas lamps. There are no entrées on the menu (and no gruel), just small plates, but, oh, what glorious snacks they are! We always ask for more, particularly of the blue-cheese-and-bacon-stuffed dates, garlic truffled popcorn, and mini-grilled-cheese sandwich with frothy tomato "cappuccino." They offer several beers (only one from Blighty) and a pleasing wine list, but we love the drinks, especially those named for Fagin and the Artful Dodger. Cozy back tables are prime kissing territory. *$$; AE, MC, V; no checks; dinner every day; full bar; no reservations; www.oliverstwistseattle.com.*

Patit Creek Restaurant

725 E Dayton Ave, Dayton, WA; 509/382-2625

When it comes to romance, Patit Creek soars off the charts. If you are looking for an intimate moment in a charming little town to enjoy after a day of winery hopping, stop your search here. Just 30 minutes east of Walla Walla in the town of Dayton lies one of the most highly rated restaurants this side of the mountains. By the way, when we say intimate, we mean *small* as well as romantic: the restaurant, housed in a 1920s service station, has only 10 tables. The focus is French classic cuisine with a wine list strong on Walla Walla selections. All ingredients are incredibly fresh, and the huckleberry pie for dessert is a must. Make reservations at least two weeks in advance. *$$; MC, V; local checks only; lunch Wed–Fri, dinner Wed–Sat; beer and wine; reservations recommended.*

The Pink Door

1919 Post Alley, Seattle, WA; 206/443-3241

Depending upon when you go, a visit to this enduringly popular Italian-American restaurant can feel more like you've stumbled into a Fellini film than a meal. In the evenings, cabaret-style entertainment can include a trapeze artist suspended from the dim and slightly gothic dining room's 20-foot ceiling, a tarot card reader, a tap-dancing saxophonist, and burlesque shows staged in the crowded bar. On warm afternoons, a meal under the arbor on the deck is a quintessential Seattle experience. Some people come for the ambience, but with a talented chef in the kitchen, the cuisine — drawing on the bounty of the region — can be regarded as the Main Event. *$$–$$$; AE, DIS, MC, V; no checks; lunch Mon–Sat, dinner every day; full bar; reservations recommended; www.thepinkdoor.net.*

The Place Bar & Grill

1 Spring St, Friday Harbor, WA; 360/378-8707

You can cruise in here for a quick bite before you catch your ferry, but why not stay awhile? A far better plan is to enjoy a quiet dinner at this waterfront eatery. The three walls of windows at this restaurant perched on pilings — the oldest building still standing on the island — give diners excellent views of the ferry terminal and marina. Chef/owner Steven Anderson features a rotating menu of Northwest cuisine, focusing on local and regional fish and shellfish, from British Columbia king salmon to Westcott Bay oysters. Giant Alaskan weathervane scallops might arrive in a pool of ginger-lime beurre blanc; black bean ravioli could come topped with tequila shrimp. A full-service bar blends in nicely with the decor and offers plentiful options for romantic libations. *$$; MC, V; local checks only; dinner Tues–Sat (closed January; call for seasonal closures); full bar; reservations recommended; www.theplacesanjuan.com.*

Place Pigalle

81 Pike St, Seattle, WA; 206/624-1756

More than a quarter century ago, a dive bar beneath a former bordello was transformed into this atmospheric French-inspired cafe, and it has lost none of its charm to the passage of time. It boasts creamy walls, a black-and-white floor, candles on tables, a tiny bar specializing in unusual spirits, a picture-postcard view of Elliott Bay, and Edith Piaf's music playing in the background. (Wooden bistro chairs, best for petite derrières, are the only compromise to comfort.) The wine list offers modestly priced domestic and European bottles, and the menu spotlights classic preparations of rabbit, lamb, duck, and the house signature Mussels Pigalle, flavored with bacon. What makes this meal even more intimate? Patrons are asked to turn off their cell phones. *La vie* is, indeed, *rose*. *$$–$$$; AE, DC, DIS, MC, V; no checks; lunch, dinner Mon–Sat; full bar; reservations recommended; www.placepigalle-seattle.com.*

Quattro at Whistler

4319 Main St (Whistler Pinnacle Hotel), Whistler, B.C.; 604/905-4844

Enjoying good food in good company, with a steady flow of wine and conversation and a commitment to living with *abbondanza* (Italian for "the passion of poetry and life") — what better way to enjoy a romantic evening in Whistler? Although everything on the menu is out-of-this-world, the Spaghetti Quattro is especially beloved. Adventurous couples who are in the mood to indulge should consider ordering *L'Abbuffata*, the chef's famous five-course Roman feast. Finish with a glass of *vin santo* — with biscotti for dipping. *$$$$; AE, MC, V; no checks; dinner every day (high season), dinner Tues–Sat (low season); full bar; reservations recommended; www.quattrorestaurants.com.*

Serafina Osteria & Enoteca

2043 Eastlake Ave E, Seattle, WA; 206/323-0807

Low lighting, soft live jazz, and an Italian-influenced menu make any night at Serafina undeniably romantic. While the room does get busy and the small tables are set close together, the cozy ambience makes it a favored Seattle destination for intimate dates. On weekends, the atmosphere can be clamorous and the service rushed, but the ever-changing lineup of music, from Afro-Cuban to Latin, keeps the mood upbeat and festive. If it's a romantic mood you're after, Serafina won't disappoint—and warm weather dining on the outdoor patio is sublime. *$$; MC, V; checks OK; lunch Mon–Fri, dinner every day; full bar; reservations recommended; www.serafinaseattle.com.*

Silverwater Café

237 Taylor St, Port Townsend, WA; 360/385-6448

Local artwork and brick walls lend character to this little café's dining room, as do the high ceiling, numerous hanging plants, hardwood floors, and unadorned wood tables. Everything here is made from scratch, and the menu's range is surprisingly wide: The lemon baked brie with sautéed mushrooms and red onions is perfect for a light lunch, and the seafood is consistently fresh and fabulous. One especially inventive and wonderful dish is the Oysters Bleu: fresh oysters, bacon, and spinach in a light blue cheese sauce, presented on fresh black pepper linguine. It may be lacking in traditional romantic ambience, but after a beautiful day by the water, this is a distinctly warm and inviting spot to settle in for a tasty meal. *$$; MC, V; checks OK; lunch, dinner every day; full bar; reservations recommended.*

Sixth Street Bistro & Loft

509 Cascade Ave, Hood River, OR; 541/386-5737

Skip and Go Naked, a vodka, rum, and brandy concoction, will definitely set the pace for you at this "older sister" of nearby Celilo Restaurant that offers a more casual and lively atmosphere but still plenty of space to snuggle into your own conversation. The menu changes regularly and emphasizes sustainable and organic foods with a wide range of choices, from chipotle-lime chicken to oyster dishes to local favorites that include pad Thai, curries, teriyaki, and stir-fries. If you're looking for a pleasing standard, they've got a Damn Good Cheeseburger. Whatever you do, save space for house-made desserts—sure winners include crème brûlée and seasonal cobblers big enough to share. *$$–$$$; AE, DIS, MC, V; checks OK; lunch, dinner every day; full bar; reservations recommended; www.sixthstreetbistro.com.*

Sybaris

442 SW 1st St, Albany, OR; 541/928-8157

In ancient Greece, the city of Sybaris was synonymous with luxury and pleasure. So it is with this elegant restaurant on Albany's historic First Street. The charming restaurant boasts exposed brick and large windows, high ceilings, and an English-style wood-burning fireplace. Back in the kitchen, chef/owner Matt Bennett and his wife, Janel, create rotating menus that reflect a fearless and playful approach to food. Inventive options might include a "build-it-yourself little shrimp salad" with radishes, chopped herbs, hard-boiled eggs, and lemony mayo, or seared venison loin with homemade honey bacon, grilled asparagus, cracked pepper–cheese bread pudding and balsamic caramelized onions. Bennett relies on local farms for many of his ingredients and plans his monthly menus according to what's in season. The generous entrée portions may lead you to pass on dessert—which would be a shame, for you'd miss the Sybaris chocolate-hazelnut cake, a dense, flourless, decadent work of art filled with a cache of crème brûlée. The wine list is short but well matched to the menu. Monteith Riverpark is just across the street; extend the evening's pleasure with a starlit stroll by the river. *$$–$$$; AE, MC, V; checks OK; dinner Tues–Sat; full bar; reservations recommended; www.sybarisbistro.com.*

Taverna Tagaris

844 Tulip Ln, Richland, WA; 509/628-0020

Greek-influenced Tagaris offers romance paired with good food and wine. The dining room and wine bar are a mix of warm colors and hard elements (metals and concrete). Dinner favorites include Goat Cheese Tortelli paired with 04 Chardonnay, and Apple-Wood Grilled Misty Isle Beef paired with 01 Cabernet Sauvignon. The Ooey Gooey Chocolate Bomb and the Caramel Apple Flatbread are must-haves. During summer (May–Sept), the spacious patio opens, featuring a 33-foot fountain—a wonderful reprieve from warm temperatures, not to mention a cool place to steal a kiss. The patio offers casual dining and live music. Tagaris Winery is an estate winery producing both reds and whites. *$$–$$$; AE, MC, V; no checks; lunch, dinner Mon–Sat, tasting room 11am–5pm every day; full bar; www.tagariswines.com.*

Trellis Restaurant

220 Kirkland Ave (the Heathman Hotel), Kirkland, WA; 425/284-5900

"Farm to table" is an increasingly popular concept, but few chefs embrace it as whole-heartedly as Brian Scheehser, who sustainably farms 3 acres and "puts up" all manner of lush produce so that Trellis guests can enjoy the fruits of his labors year-round. If a booth isn't available in the casually elegant dining room, sit in the sleek bar (sipping cucumber Cosmos and pineapple-sage Mojitos) or on the heated patio, weather allowing. It's hard to play favorites with Scheehser's best-of-the-season dishes, but at breakfast, look for house-made corned-beef hash with poached eggs and hollandaise, and at lunch, wild salmon niçoise salad. For dinner try Sonoma duck with braised endive, grilled pears, and figs. *$$$; AE, DC, DIS, MC, V; no checks; breakfast, dinner every day, lunch Mon–Fri; full bar; reservations recommended; www.trellisrestaurant.net.*

T's Restaurant

2320 Washington St, Port Townsend, WA; 360/385-0700

This local favorite has relaxed elegance, Mediterranean ambience, and outstanding food. Tawny stucco walls; soft lighting; a crackling fire; and tables and booths set with crisp white linens, olive oil, and flowers help set the mood for a memorable evening. Signature specials include apple-wood bacon-wrapped king salmon and rack of lamb served with horseradish and new potatoes. The refined setting, distinctive and well-executed menu, top-quality service, and flawless presentations make this a perfect choice for a special night out. *$$–$$$; AE, MC, V; checks OK; dinner Wed–Mon; beer and wine; reservations recommended; www. ts-restaurant.com.*

Tulio Ristorante

1100 5th Ave (Hotel Vintage Park), Seattle, WA; 206/624-5500

This bustling Italian trattoria has a warm and intimate air, with the scent of roasted garlic, a wood-burning oven, and an open kitchen evoking the atmosphere of an entirely welcoming Tuscan villa. Menus change every day or two, reflecting the seasons and chef Walter Pisano's imagination; you might delight in calamari grilled with lavender sausage and chick-peas; chanterelle mushroom risotto; or duck breast with crispy confit, braised brussels sprouts, and golden raisins, scented with orange zest. Focaccia, gelati, granitas, and desserts (the chocolate pudding cake's a local favorite) are all made fresh on the premises daily. Service is swift, knowledgeable, and attentive. *$$; AE, DC, DIS, JCB, MC, V; no checks; breakfast, lunch, dinner every day; full bar; reservations recommended; www.tulio.com.*

ROMANTIC WINERIES

Bonair Winery & Vineyards

500 S Bonair Rd, Zillah, WA; 509/829-6027

This bright yellow French Riviera–style winery in Rattlesnake Hills recently opened a new tasting room and is said to "accommodate lovers." The most romantic spot is a bench near the koi pond. The grassy area is shaded by bamboo, which borders the canal on the other side. The grounds are a lovely place for a picnic, a glass of wine, or a marriage proposal, if you're so inclined. Wine goddess Shirley Puryear is full of fun, amorous stories and might even be coaxed into telling about the bamboo room . . . mmm-hmm. The tasting room is open 10am–5pm every day. After 5pm, the winery can accommodate weddings up to 75 guests. During tasting hours, Bonair Bistro serves *tapas* and other delights. *10am–5pm every day (Sat–Sun only Jan–Feb); www.bonairwine.com.*

Bookwalter Winery

894 Tulip Ln, Richland, WA; 509/627-5000 or 877/667-8300

Bookwalter is an intimate lounge-style sanctuary. The Tasting Room is connected by a corridor to the smaller, cozier lounge, which is adjoined to the Garden Room. This outdoor living room is full of comfy furniture and encircled by more than 100 species of roses. Walk the paths through the gardens, where you can find a little more privacy among the coves of flowers. The Tasting Room features tall cocktail tables while the connected lounge presents comfortable sofas and oversize chairs. Red velvet drapes the windows against rich Tuscan-shaded walls. The menu includes artisan cheese samplers, small plates, light fare, meats, and desserts. Tasting Room hours are 10am–6pm, then live music takes the stage 4 or 5 nights a week. Check the Web site for details on current lineups. *$–$$; AE, DIS, MC, V; checks OK; www.bookwalterwines.com.*

Cor Cellars

151 Old Hwy 8, Lyle, WA; 509/365-2744

Cor Cellars' first passion may be wine, but its second is affairs of the heart. Named after the Latin word for "heart" and founded upon the motto "Good wine pleases the human heart," the winery undeniably caters to lovers of wine and romance. Kissable opportunities abound from the moment visitors are guided along a poppy- and sunflower-lined pathway to the tasting room that awaits filled with French oak barrels and seductive smells. After sampling the winery's five wines, lovers be sure to stroll to the top of the winery's hill (with each other and wine in hand, of course!), where the Columbia River is visible for miles in both directions and the majestic Mt. Hood stands. Keep in mind, tasting fees are waived after purchasing a bottle and tours available upon request. *11am–6pm Wed–Sun, or by appointment; www.corcellars.com.*

Dunham Cellars

150 E Boeing Ave, Walla Walla, WA; 509/529-4685

Housed in a WWII airplane hangar near the airport, Dunham Cellars is a simple, welcoming gathering place. The grounds are landscaped, perfect for a stroll or picnic, and there's plenty of canine love to go around with the three iconic Dunham winery dogs. The tasting room abuts the larger part of the newly renovated hangar. High ceilings create an open, airy feel, while comfy sitting areas carved out of the vast space make it cozy and inviting. Cuddle up with a glass of wine, a loaf of homemade bread, and salami or cheese available at the winery; or admire winemaker and artist Eric Dunham's original art. For a secret place to kiss, ask to see the doghouse. *11am–4pm every day; www.dunhamcellars.com.*

King Estate Winery

80854 Territorial Rd, Eugene, OR; 541/942-9874

Situated just a short drive away from Eugene through rolling country-side, this established winery offers spectacular views and award-winning wines. Steal a moment while wandering through the barrel room, or in warmer weather, sip a glass of signature chardonnay on one of three secluded patios (our favorite is hidden away in the pear orchard). Enjoy the winery's spacious tasting room and a restaurant that serves lunch and dinner daily. Ingredients for its farm-fresh cuisine hail from the estate's organic farm. Highlights include a plentiful artisan cheese plate adorned with sweet wine grapes; a light baby Belgian endive salad served with candied walnuts, Oregon blue cheese, and a delicate orange cham-pagne vinaigrette; and roasted chicken served over wild mushrooms, baby Yukon potatoes, and sautéed greens. Or, come for an indulgent dessert of cinnamon crème brûlée or an apricot *tartine* as the sun descends behind the surrounding hills of this spectacular hilltop winery. *11am–8pm every day; www.kingestate.com.*

Quails' Gate Estate Winery

3303 Boucherie Rd, Kelowna, B.C.; 250/769-4451 or 800/420-9463

Quails' Gate can trace its roots all the way back to the early 1900s, when the Stewart family was in the tree fruit business. The delightful setting boasts an early–20th century log-house tasting room and an exquisite vineyard that tumbles down the property to Okanagan Lake. The Old Vines Patio, open May to October, is a magical spot for a late dinner on a summer night; it offers fresh, seasonal cuisine and a panoramic view that has encouraged more than one prairie couple to consider a move and career change. Burgundy-style pinot noir and chardonnay are the focus at Quails' Gate, but don't miss an opportunity to taste their chenin blanc, chasselas, or dry Riesling. The winery has also developed a cult following for its Old Vines Foch, a shiraz-style blockbuster red that is rarely seen outside the winery. *10am–5pm every day (extended hours in summer); www.quailsgate.com*

Torii Mor Winery

18325 NE Fairview Dr, Dundee, OR; 503/538-2279 or 800/839-5004
Dust off from the drive up the long gravel road that leads to this hidden hillside winery and enter its peaceful Japanese garden—complete with a small rock garden and grassy alcoves. Torii Mor's growing popularity means you'll likely share sipping space in the minimalist Japanese-style tasting room and garden with other oenophiles in search of remarkable pinot noirs. Enjoy a tasting flight of the winery's high-end wines then steal a private moment while wandering through the adjacent vineyards. *11am–5pm every day; www.toriimorwinery.com.*

Vin du Lac Winery

105 Highway 150, Chelan, WA; 509/682-2882 or 800/455-9463
This winery is housed in a yellow country cottage in the midst of an orchard. The vineyards slope to the tasting room with peekaboo lake views filtering through the branches above the perennial-garden wine patio. Owners Larry Lehmbecker and Michaela Markusson have created a kind of outdoor living room—an intimate and comfy spot to slow down and watch the sun set. The small menu offers French bistro offerings, perfect in their simplicity. *Every day; www.vindulac.com.*

Index

I, J

K, L